LIGHT on QUESTS MOUNTAIN

BY MARY L. KIRCHOFF and JAMES M. WARD

A GAMMA WORLD™ ADVENTURE BOOK

Cover Art By Keith Parkinson
Interior Art by Steve McAfee

TSR, Inc.

To England,
the land from which
the best within us springs.

LIGHT ON QUESTS MOUNTAIN
©Copyright 1983, TSR, Inc.
All Rights Reserved.

Distributed to the book trade in the United States by Random House, Inc. and in Canada by Random House of Canada, Ltd.
Distributed in the United Kingdom by TSR (UK), Ltd.
Distributed to the toy and hobby trade by regional distributors.

DUNGEONS & DRAGONS, GAMMA WORLD, ENDLESS QUEST, and PICK A PATH TO ADVENTURE are trademarks owned by TSR, Inc.

D&D is a registered trademark owned by TSR, Inc.

First printing: August, 1983
Printed in the United States of America.
Library of Congress Catalog Card Number: 83-50290
ISBN: 0-88038-055-1

9 8 7 6 5 4 3 2 1

TSR, Inc.
P.O. Box 756
Lake Geneva, WI 53147

TSR (UK), Ltd.
The Mill, Rathmore Road
Cambridge CB1 4AD
United Kingdom

YOU MUST SURVIVE
IN A DEVASTATED WORLD!

In *Light on Quests Mountain,* you are Ren, a young boy living in a possible world of the future. In this world, man has been forced to live much as he did when spears and survival were a way of life. The people of this primitive society are both helped and confused by the remnants they find of a civilization far more advanced than inhabitants of the twentieth century can imagine.

Legend says that long ago, so long that no one you, as Ren, know was living then, terrible wars swept the civilized world, leaving vast wastelands where no man can live.

Before the wars began, man was ruler of the earth. But one result of these terrible wars was that creatures rose from the ashes of the bombs. The genes of the earth's animals and plants were altered, until strange, new creatures arose—creatures of awesome power and fierceness and often great intelligence.

A courageous member of your village has returned from the far north to boast of an intelligent race of lizards, which is starting to build its own civilization. Two members of a fifteen-member Southlands expedition have returned with evidence that huge machines are building a city from the ashes of an old one. Robots function in a way no man ever put into their circuits.

Villages like yours have sprung up in areas least damaged by the wars.

Man no longer rules. He must share the land. With caution and luck, he exists.

"That's it! No more school!" shouts Chark, bounding out of the brick and thatch building that serves as your school.

"I'm almost sorry to see it end," says Sars slowly. "I think I'll ask Merel if I might work as a teacher's apprentice."

"All I can think about is beginning our quest tomorrow," you say.

You are Ren, youngest son of the chief of the village of New Hope. Tomorrow, you and your two friends begin the journey that every graduate of the school must face. You must venture to Quests Mountain and face whatever dangers you encounter. Only then will you overcome your fears and be accepted as adult members of your village.

You, Sars, and Chark will have an important additional purpose on your quest. Recently, villagers have spotted a strange light atop Quests Mountain. The village elders have asked you to try to determine the source of that light.

"They sure don't waste any time, what with having us leave the very day after we graduate," Chark says dryly.

"No point in prolonging the inevitable," says Sars, always the reasonable one.

"Why does he have to talk that way?" Chark asks you.

You sigh, ignoring the question. Chark really expects no answer. Teasing each other is a game your two friends have always played. Fortunately, it is just a game.

You glance at your tall friend. Although Sars's scaly skin and features are those of a lizard, he walks like a man, and his hands and mind function as well as a human's. You've learned to take his slow, deliberate speech seriously, since he often notices things that others don't.

Sars wears his glasses—rare in your world—with pride, but they don't prevent his terrible fear of darkness. You know that he will have to try to conquer this fear if your quest is to be a success.

Your eyes stray to Chark, and you think how different your monkey friend is from Sars. Skinny, hairy Chark seldom thinks things through as Sars does. Chark has led you and Sars on many a merry adventure, but you hope he'll be more careful on your quest. Even more, you hope he'll be able to overcome his deep fear of water.

You find it hard to admit, but you are nervous at the thought of your upcoming quest. You will be the leader, and you fear making a wrong decision that might risk the lives of your friends. You come from a family of great leaders, and you wonder if you can live up to them. Your thoughts turn to Jor, your closest brother, who was to have succeeded your father as chief. The entire village mourned when he went to the desert on his quest and never returned.

With a strong effort, you snap your mind to the present. "Go home, you two, and check your gear once more. We'll meet in the village square early tomorrow morning," you say as you start to leave.

You awaken to a bright, clear morning. You check your gear one last time, hug your sisters, and set off for the square with your parents. A crowd of well-wishers has gathered there to send the three of you off on your quest.

Your father claps his hands and everyone falls silent.

"As you all know, it is our custom to send our young graduates to Quests Mountain before becoming adult members of our village.

"It is also our custom to present each young person departing on a quest with a special gift. Ren, Sars, Chark: these fine metal spears are given to you in the hope they will serve you well on your journey." One by one, you examine your spears wonderingly as they are presented. Spears with metal heads are rare enough in the village, but weapons made entirely of metal are very special indeed.

Each of you mumbles his thanks, with a promise to try to be worthy of such an extraordinary gift. Sars's mother hugs him impulsively, and he blushes deeply, his green skin turning murky brown.

Your father speaks once more. "Go now, young ones. Return to us as proud men."

With the words of your father ringing in your ears, you set off for the main gate of the village. Once outside the village, the three of you pause to talk over your plans. You've discussed your quest many times, but even now, at the last minute, you're still debating your course of action.

"I say we head straight north, right for the mountain," says Chark.

"Chark, you know the Great Northern Wastelands stretch between our village and Quests Mountain. And you know that no one who has entered the Wastelands has ever returned," Sars reminds him.

"Sars is right," you say. "We must go around the Wastelands."

"But which way?" asks Chark. "If we head east, we must pass through the Sand Lands. The dunes of the Sand Lands conceal many hidden dangers. If we head west, we must travel through the Green Lands. Fearsome creatures are said to inhabit the forests and foothills of the Green Lands."

"Ren, didn't your brother Jor head through the desert?" Sars asks.

"He said he was going to, but we don't really know for sure."

Chark fidgets. "The trail through the Green Lands is shorter. Let's go that way."

"But it might be interesting to retrace Jor's steps," Sars says thoughtfully.

"Perhaps," you say, trying to weigh the advantages of each route.

Straight ahead, dust and decayed bones mark the beginning of the Great Northern Wastelands.

To the west, you see the leafy roof of the

dangerous Green Lands. Turning to the east, you face the perilous Sand Lands, the path your brother followed.

It is time to decide. Which way will you lead your friends?

1) If you decide to journey through the Sand Lands to reach your destination, turn to page 28.

2) If you would rather travel through the Green Lands to reach the mountain, turn to page 51.

"Let's explore the cave," you decide, nudging Chark as you pass him.

Chark, lost in thoughts about how to politely refuse a meal of small, furry rodents, hasn't heard a word.

"Come on, you lazy monkey, we're going exploring." Chark comes to his senses and joins you. You find some torches in brackets on the wall just inside the cave entrance, and you each light one.

Inside the cave, you quickly come upon a shallow, murky stream. In the middle of the stream stand a number of stone statues. The edges of some are worn smooth by the flowing water.

"I wonder how they got here," muses Sars, echoing your own thoughts.

The heat from the torches in the dampness of the cave has turned the air hot and sultry. You notice that Sars's glasses have fogged over. You see him stumble, alarmingly close to the bank of the stream.

"Be careful, Sars. It's pretty slippery here," you caution him, running a sandaled foot gingerly over a slime-covered rock.

Standing back a bit from the edge, Chark leans over and peers into the water. He begins to say, "Hey, I think there are fish—" Suddenly Sars loses his footing and slides into the stream. Instantly his torch goes out with a hiss.

You dash to the edge of the stream to find Sars, but instead you see large, fierce-looking fish. They're erts! Their bite turns their victims to stone!

"Sars, get out of the water! Hurry!" you yell, thrusting your hand out to him.

Sars seems unable to get his bearings. He flails his arms helplessly. "Help!" he pants weakly.

Sizing up the situation instantly, Chark dives into the water and swims desperately upstream against the strong current toward Sars. In horror you see that it has become a race between Chark and the erts.

Chark catches at Sars's arm as he gropes in panic. For a moment, the helpless lizard fights the monkey boy. Then fear for both of them gives Chark the extra strength to overcome Sars's struggles, and he pulls Sars toward the bank. From shore, you see a large ert coming up fast just behind Sars's heels. You pick up a rock and hurl it at the ert with all your might, but it misses.

Finally Chark shoves Sars to the bank. You reach out and grab Sars under the arms and pull him up onto the bank. Chark's feet clear the water just in time, and there is a terrible crunch as the ert's savage jaws snap closed, only inches behind your monkey friend.

Exhausted, you drop onto your knees next to Sars.

"I'm sorry," he finally says after he gets his breath. "I couldn't see very well, what with my glasses fogged. Thank you, Chark."

Chark rolls his eyes and quickly changes

the subject. "Where are your glasses, Sars?"

Sars puts a hand up to his face. "I don't know. . . . They must have fallen off in the water."

The three of you hunt for the glasses, all the while keeping a constant lookout for more erts. But it's soon clear that the glasses are gone forever.

"Well, that settles it," you say resignedly. "We've got to return home. We can't lead Sars day and night. At least, each of us has come a long way toward conquering his fears."

Your friends look both pleased and sad at the same time.

"We can return another time to discover the cause of the light at the top of Quests Mountain. But now, let us proudly return to our village as men of New Hope."

THE END

"It will be difficult for Sars to move in the dark, but I think we must go," you say. "It's very dangerous here."

Not liking to be a burden, Sars notes, "The desert will be very hot during the day. We can make more progress in the cool of the night."

"Then it's settled. I'll help guide Sars. Chark, you scout a little way ahead of us and look for anything of interest. I really don't think we'll have to face many more of these hills before we reach the real desert. The air feels warmer and drier already," you say.

"You mean this isn't it?" asks Chark, horrified.

"No, Chark, this is only the beginning. The desert itself is much flatter and sandier," answers Sars.

Shrugging, Chark skips ahead.

Soon you say, "Brrr. The wind is getting stronger."

"Yes, I'm getting a lot of sand in my eyes," says Sars, rubbing at his glasses with the back of a scaly hand.

"And I'm getting a lot in my mouth," says Chark, spitting. "But I haven't seen any rocks or boulders for a while. We're definitely in the desert now—my sandals are filled with sand, and it's slowing me down. The sand's cool enough now for bare feet," he says, slipping his shoes off and stuffing them in his pack. You and Sars remove yours, too.

With sandals off, you walk faster. Chark skips farther ahead. Trudging through the sand in silence, you each think your own thoughts.

The burden of leading your friends is beginning to weigh heavily. You wonder if you have made the right decision, moving on in the darkness. Is it putting too great a strain on Sars?

To his surprise, Sars has begun to enjoy your night trek. At first slowed and frightened by the dark, he has begun to trust his friends—and to use his other four senses more. He is amazed and delighted with the number of things he notices without the use of his eyes.

"Can you smell that?" he asks you and Chark.

"All I smell is sand and more sand!" says Chark.

"No, there's a very strong fragrance coming from up ahead," he insists.

You see Chark's thin shoulders raise in a shrug as he walks on.

Unaccustomed to walking in sand, your leg muscles soon tire. You long to stop, but know that you need to keep moving in the cool night air.

Just when you think you can walk no farther, the sun's rays begin to show above the horizon. Soon you see a small patch of trees and a pool of dull black water that seems to brighten with each step you take.

"An oasis! This must be what you were smelling, Sars. At least we won't have to

worry about water for a while," you say, skipping past a ring of tall, cactuslike plants to the
water's edge.

"This will be a great place to rest, too," says
Sars. "I'm feeling every wound from those
awful nightwings!"

You bend over and cup your hand into the
water. Behind you, you hear Chark gasp. You
swirl around. The tall plants are moving
closer! Your eyes widen at what you see—
they're wearing saddles!

You shake your head to clear your tired
eyes. But the saddled cactuses are still there.

Then Sars exclaims, "They're pinetos, Ren!
My father told me that when he was young, he
used to tame and ride them. He said that they
only do well in deserts like this, which is why
we don't have them in our village." He stops
for a moment, a puzzled look on his face. "But
they no longer run free, so these must have
escaped from their masters recently. Hey,
maybe we can catch them by their head vines
and ride them through the desert."

Knowing that the pinetos must be fairly
tame, each of you runs up to one and grabs the
vines that hang from its headstalk. The rest of
the pinetos run away into the desert.

"This is great!" says Chark, climbing up on
his mount. He fiddles around and quickly gets
the hang of the control sticks at the top of the
headstalk. The plants move in a steady, plod-
ding fashion and seem quite comfortable to
sit on.

"Let's hurry and try these things out in the desert," Chark prompts.

"Wait a minute, Chark," says Sars. "We haven't studied this oasis. We're not likely to run into another, and there could be many interesting things here."

Your friends look at you for a decision.

1) Will you rest for a while and study the oasis? Turn to page 104.

2) Or will you take advantage right away of finding the pinetos and head out into the desert? Turn to page 100.

You hear your father's voice saying, "A leader knows when to act and when to wait for a better opportunity." And you know that, as much as you want to dash to Jor's aid, you must think things through.

Shifting slightly to avoid several rocks digging into your stomach, you notice that the whole area around you is strewn with rocks. You point out that fact to Sars and Chark beside you.

"I've been wondering about that," says Sars. "I think we're in the old drybed of the river. The badders must have shifted it for some reason."

"I have a plan," you announce. "It's dangerous but not as dangerous as racing straight into the village. We're going to break the dam and send all that water rushing through the village."

"And what are we going to do about the badders guarding the dam? Say, 'Excuse us while we break your dam?'" asks Chark. "And what about Jor and the other prisoners?"

"We'll get rid of the badders guarding the dam somehow. And I don't think there's enough water to harm the prisoners, but the badders all live below ground. Didn't you notice their holes? We'll wait until it gets darker and then go to the lake," you say.

"In that case, someone will have to lead me," Sars reminds you. "It's not too bad here near the firelight, but I'd be almost blind by the lake."

"You can stay behind and listen and tell us if any more badders are coming. We'll probably have to cross the lake to get to the dam. Chark will come with me."

"Uh . . . maybe we'd better wait," says Chark, his eyes widening at mention of water.

"We can't wait. And we must do it tonight," you insist.

Chark hesitates. You can almost hear his inner struggle. "I'll—I'll go. But let's do it now, before I lose my nerve."

Leading your lizard friend, you retrace your steps through the forest and along the riverbed to the lake.

"Look! There's only one guard," whispers Chark.

"Yeah, and his back is to us," you say. "It'll make it easier for us to sneak up behind him."

Leaving Sars at the edge of the forest, you and Chark slowly, silently creep along the edge of the river, through the clearing, and around the dam to the lake. With a quick glance at Chark, you enter the chilly water. You hear Chark whimper slightly as he follows you and slides in. You pat his shoulder encouragingly.

You paddle soundlessly toward the badder guard, your heart pounding. As you near the back of the dam, you seek the lake bottom with a toe and discover that it slopes gradually upward toward the dam. You hear Chark let out a deep breath when he feels firm ground once more.

Looking up, you see that the guard stands relaxed, leaning on its club. You signal Chark, and you each grab one of the guard's furry legs and pull with all your might.

"What the—" it growls, confused. The guard tries to catch its balance, at the same time reaching for its sword. With another sharp tug, the badder tumbles into the water.

"Stay away from its teeth!" you hiss at Chark. You watch, horrified, as the badder snaps at Chark.

"No, you don't!" you holler, bringing your fist down squarely on the crown of the badder's head. You swing again, and the guard slumps over in the water and floats off, facedown, until it bumps headfirst into the lower wall of the reservoir.

"Whew!" you sigh, and rush over to where Chark is hanging on to the bank. Just then you hear a cry from the other side of the lake.

Sars! You look up to see him grappling with another badder!

You swim madly through the water, only to be met by the body of the second badder as it topples into the water, trailing blood. Worried, you look up and see your friend, a look of satisfaction on his lizard face.

"Sars, what happened?" you whisper.

"Another one of those filthy things leaped out of the forest. You two were busy, so..." His voice trails off.

You haul yourself out of the water beside Sars. "I'd hate to see what you could do to a badder when you can see him," you marvel.

When Chark joins you, you say urgently, "We don't know if more badders are on the way. We've got to hurry and break the dam."

You start chopping at the logs and stones of the dam with your spears. In a short time, you hear a loud creaking noise. You chip out a few more stones, then yell, "Stand back! It's going to go!" The rest of the dam gives way with a loud crash, and the river floods into its old pathway, sweeping the bodies of the badders along with it.

"No time to celebrate," you say. "We've got to get to Jor."

You grab Sars's arm and trot to a higher spot, away from the river. You leave him waiting at the edge of the forest, beyond the flow of water.

You and Chark dash to the village and arrive just in time to see the water snuff out the last remnant of the fire, leaving only moonlight to see by.

Sleepy badders, shouting in confusion and fear, scramble up ladders from their rapidly filling dens.

You and Chark slosh through the village to a hut near the prisoner cage. The badders are too busy to notice you.

"Come on, Chark! Now's our chance!" You hurry around the hut to the door of the cage. The prisoners stare out from behind the bars at the scene of confusion. Some scream in fear as water laps at their legs.

"Jor?" you whisper, searching into the mass of faces.

"Who's there?" You see Jor's tall, thin body pushing through the crowd.

"Jor! It's me, Ren!"

"Ren? No . . . it can't be. Is it really you?"

You begin to hack and pry at the wooden gate with your spear. Soon you have cleared an opening big enough to crawl through. Prisoners begin to scramble out hastily. Finally, the scraggy form of your brother emerges through the opening, and you throw your arms about him.

"Ren! It is you! I can't believe it," he says, joy lighting his thin face.

Reluctant to release you, Jor holds your shoulders and stands back a bit. "You've changed—become a man. But how did you get here?"

"Let's get away from here first," you say. "The water's getting higher. And I'm sure your badder hosts aren't exactly happy with us for rerouting their river."

"So YOU did this! Same old Ren," he says, wiping his eyes with the back of his hand.

"Let's go," you say gruffly, afraid of the swelling in your throat.

"Chark!" he exclaims as Chark moves into the moonlight.

"Sars is waiting for us by the trees south of the village—or what was the village," you add, looking around at the collapsing huts.

The three of you slosh through the water

we should go through the desert to ___ntaintop," you say to your friends. ___ thought that you might find some trace of your brother Jor makes your heart leap with excitement.

"Okay," says Chark quickly. "It doesn't matter to me, just as long as we get going." With that he skips off toward the northeast and the low range of hills that hides the beginnings of the desert.

"I worry about Chark," says Sars, watching your monkey friend. "Sometimes he's too quick for his own good. We'll both have to watch him and make sure he doesn't get into trouble."

Sars chuckles and continues. "I hope he gives us time to enjoy the areas we travel through. I never saw anyone move so fast and see so little!"

"Funny you should say that, Sars," you say, laughing. "Chark just told me that he never saw anybody move so slow and see so much!" You both laugh and run to catch up with Chark.

Soon your lizard friend says, "It's odd that I don't recognize a single plant."

"There aren't very many of them, either," adds Chark.

"Look at this!" Sars exclaims, bending over a purple bush with orange, cone-shaped flowers. "Can you hear those bells?" he asks, face aglow with excitement. "The wind makes the flowers on the bush ring."

A gentle breeze swirls around you, setting the bells to chiming.

"Why does it do that?" Chark asks.

"Probably to frighten away birds or bats that might eat the berries," says Sars. "But it's a nice sound, too," he adds.

The wind picks up in the late afternoon. The farther you move into the dry desert, the fewer and stranger the plants become.

You stop once to eat but continue walking until near sunset.

"We should look for a campsite for the night," you shout to Chark, who is climbing some large rocks off the path.

Chark looks longingly at the next ledge, shrugs, and then shouts down, "Let's make for those big rocks way up ahead! I can climb them in the morning and scout out the best path to take through these hills."

You walk on, collecting small sticks and dried weeds, which you use to make a fire in the shelter of the boulders.

Gradually darkness closes in around you.

"How are you holding up, Sars?" you ask your lizard friend.

"Oh, I'm all right if I stay within the light of the fire. I have to count on my other senses at night, and sometimes they just aren't good enough." He hesitates and then adds, "Sometimes I envy you and Chark."

"I know what you mean, Sars," says Chark. "I've often wanted to be able to smell as well as Surell, the village elder, or to hear as well as his wife, Dasandra." He sighs and plops down in a heap before the fire.

After a few moments, he leans forward and points toward the outline of the moon. "Why, I bet Dasandra would have heard the beating of those wings up there long before this."

"Wings? What wings?" You look up quickly, scanning the sky.

Suddenly, as the last rays of the sun fall below the horizon, you see black-winged creatures flying in your direction. Hundreds of the birdlike things flap loudly in the violet-blue sky.

"They look just like nightwings!" you shout above the noise.

"Yes, but they're so huge—much bigger than the ones around our village," says Chark.

Just as suddenly as they appeared, the black-winged creatures start to dive straight at you! You each pull out your spear and try to jab at them, but they are too quick. They nip at your bodies, then dart off.

"Get away! Get away!" you hear the lizard boy shout, panic in his voice.

Sars is having more trouble than you. Even with the light of the fire, it's impossible for him to see their dark bodies against the night sky. For each creature he manages to hit, two more fall on him, beaks pecking viciously.

"Chark! Get on the other side of Sars. We must guard each other's backs.

"These can't be nightwings!" you shout. "They're too big!"

"They're black, mostly wing, and come out at dusk—that makes them nightwings! And that makes us supper!" Chark yells as he withdraws his spear from one.

"I can't see them!" cries Sars, numb from the pain and frustration of the nightwings' ceaseless attacks.

You move closer to Sars in hope of relieving him a little, but there are so many creatures in the darkness that you have all you can do to save yourself.

"These spears just aren't working!" you shout. "We aren't hitting enough of them!" Two nightwings dodge around your flailing spear and bite you on the arm and leg.

"I can't even feel my arms anymore!" cries Sars, so angered and humiliated that he begins to shout at the bats in rage.

"Get away from me. Goooooooo!" he roars.

You look at the usually calm lizard boy in surprise.

Just as startled, the nightwings suddenly miss their targets. They begin to crash into rocks, ram each other in midflight, and even fly straight into the ground!

A smile spreads over your face. "Keep yelling! It seems to hurt them!"

You and Chark join Sars in yelling any gibberish that comes to mind, as long as it's loud. The creatures become even more confused and gradually fly away. Soon every one of the batlike things has either flown away or is dead on the ground around you.

Chark lets out a "Whoopee!" and hops cir-
cles around Sars.

"You've won the battle for us, Sars!" you
shout, slapping your lizard friend on the back.
Sars smiles, embarrassed but grateful.

But then your joy gives way to pain as you
each begin to feel the effects of the deep cuts
the creatures made on your bodies.

There are dead nightwings all over. Some
have fallen into the fire and smell terrible as
they burn.

"There's a good chance that we haven't
seen the last of those giant nightwings," you
say thoughtfully. "Some of them may smell
these dead ones and come looking for a free
meal. After we clean our wounds, we'd better
decide what to do.

1) "We could keep traveling now when the
   desert is cool." Turn to page 16.

2) "Maybe the desert is just too dangerous
   and we should retrace our steps and go
   through the Green Lands to reach
   Quests Mountain." Turn to page 84.

3) "Or should we stay near the protection
   of these rocks for the night and decide
   what to do in the morning?" Turn to
   page 68.

"Let's go in the lower opening and take the pinetos with us. We shouldn't leave them out in the hot sun. They're a bit wilted as it is," you say.

You lead your pineto to the opening, lean in, and peer slowly in all directions.

The sun shining a little way through the opening shows only sand and dust covering the floor. There are no tracks in the wind-blown sand, no signs of anyone or anything having been here recently. You breathe easier.

"It looks safe," you say and slowly extend a foot into the body of the airplane.

Reassured, Chark pushes past you and boldly steps in.

"Of course it's safe," he says. Sars shrugs, pushes up his glasses to get a better look at the inside, and follows Chark.

Suddenly, from the darkness above, blanket-like flying forms drop down on you. In an instant their gooey, fleshly folds have smothered you and your mounts. You have only a brief moment to regret the outcome of your quest.

THE END

"Run!" you shout to your friends. You run by the tree and sprint down the path, your friends in close pursuit. An arrow thuds to the ground between you and Chark, missing you both narrowly.

"Wow!" he puffs.

"Just keep running," you yell sharply. You run until your sides ache. Finally you glance back. No one seems to be following.

"I . . . think . . . we can stop," you puff.

You fall to your knees on the path, pull your water container from your pack, and drink deeply. Then you let your body fall backward to the ground, and you stare through the purple trees at the blue sky above while you catch your wind.

You hear your friends begin to move around. Suddenly Chark shouts, "Hey, you two! I found something—a cave!"

You sit up and look around. "Where are you, Chark?"

"Over here," his voice calls back.

You follow the voice down a path to a clearing.

"See?" says Chark, pointing at a large hole in the side of the mountain.

You look through the opening and see a vast tunnel, apparently leading straight into the mountain. "Hmmmm. This might be a good place for us to spend the night. It'll be dark in a couple of hours."

"I don't know . . ." Sars says hesitantly. "It'll be real dark in there."

"It'll be real dark out here, too!" Chark reminds him impatiently.

"Yes, but have you ever been in TOTAL darkness? Even you two won't be able to see," Sars says.

"Dark is dark," Chark says with a shrug.

"No . . . Sars is right," you say. "None of us can see in there. We're going to have to find some way to light the cave."

"I have something," Sars says sheepishly. He pulls his pack from his scaly back, reaches in, and takes out a large cube-shaped object.

"I wanted to keep it a secret because you were so fussy about our equipment lists, but I sneaked it along anyway. This is a glow cube." Then he adds in a rush, "I didn't want to bring it, but my parents insisted. I guess they were just trying to help." He stops and hangs his head.

"We understand, Sars," you say. "As it turns out, we really need it."

Sars's face brightens. "Yeah?" he says.

"So how does it work?" asks Chark.

"You break the glass enclosure on one of the four sections to activate the light. It'll glow with a blue light for about one night."

"Well, are we going into the cave or aren't we?" Chark asks impatiently.

"Yes, but only to see if it's safe to spend the night there. No running off alone to explore."

You lead the way through the tunnel entrance. Ten paces in, sunlight gives way to darkness.

"All right. Break the cube," you say. A sharp tap is followed by the sound of breaking glass.

"Wow!" gasps Chark.

Your eyes widen at the sight of hundreds of stalactites and stalagmites bathed in the eerie blue glow.

"What a place to explore," Sars says.

"Yeah!" marvels Chark, his eyes as big as saucers.

Suddenly you glimpse sight of a form reflected in the light. "Something's in here!" you whisper, your heart pounding.

"Helllooooo!" a voice booms, echoing through the cave. "What's that in your hand, little lizard boy? Why, it's a glow cube!" The form claps its hands loudly. As the sound echoes through the tunnel, you stand motionless. You decide that the creature, whatever it is, sounds friendly.

The figure approaches the light. You gasp as you see two female heads with flowing green hair. Two sets of arms extend from a single body, and four hands are clapping again.

"Oh, my!" Sars exclaims quietly.

"This is it!" whimpers Chark, hiding his face. "I just know it!"

Sars's hand shakes violently, and the light from the glow cube flits crazily about the cavern.

"Come here, little lizard. Let the orlen see your pretty cube," one head invites silkily.

"Don't go, Sars. I bet she wants to eat you!" warns Chark.

"What should I do, Ren?" Sars asks, fear in his eyes.

1) If you think Sars should give the cube to the orlen, turn to page 61.

2) If you wish to take your chances and fight the orlen, turn to page 147.

Chark peers into the opening at the left.

"Boy, listen to that noise!" he says. He disappears inside for a moment, then pokes his head back out and says, "There seems to be a light at the end of this tunnel."

You follow Chark in and look over his shoulder, deep into the tunnel.

"I think you're right," you say. "Sars, we'll lead you until we get closer to the light." The lizard boy nods his head. You take his arm and step into the tunnel.

You can't make out what's causing the sound, but the noise gets worse with each step you take. The heat is intense.

Sars stumbles, and you hold his arm more firmly. Your eyes begin to adjust to the darkness. Is there really a light at the end of the tunnel? You're no longer sure.

You can now see that the dirt walls of the tunnel are remarkably smooth.

Suddenly you're blinded by a bright light. You close your eyes against the glare, then open them slowly behind parted fingers.

You discover that you are standing on a platform above a large room. The noise in the room is even louder than it was in the tunnel. You see now that it comes from the whirring of wheels, the clanking of metal, and the steady humming of moving metal belts. Everywhere are huge metal boxes with dials, blinking lights, and brightly lit screens. On one side of the room, you see several robots.

Your mouth drops open in wonder as you

survey the room. Chark pulls at your sleeve.

"Ren," he says through clenched teeth, "there's a man with a yellow hat over there."

"Duck!" you hiss.

Too late. You were seen.

Robots advance toward you from all sides and hustle the three of you down a staircase to where the man with the yellow hat waits on the main floor of the room. The robots leave you and disappear beyond the boxes.

"Welcome," says the man. "We don't have many visitors." Removing his metal hat, he runs a hand through thick, well-groomed white hair. Light coveralls fail to hide his tall, well-muscled frame.

"This place isn't exactly on the beaten path," says Chark with a shrug.

"May I ask what you are doing here?" inquires Sars.

"The Program must be completed," the man says without emotion.

"Program? What program?" you ask.

"The Program is the Program. It is all there is," he says simply. "The Program is nearing completion. In eighteen hours, our robots will advance on their targets. Then the cities and opposing governments will fall before us."

"What in the world is he talking about?" whispers Chark.

"I'm not sure, but he's not talking about anything in our world," you say with certainty.

"I don't like this!" exclaims Chark. "I'm getting out of here!" He turns and heads for the stairs. Two robots quickly roll to his side and force him to a stop.

You look at the tall man and realize that he is controlling the robots. You signal Sars, and the two of you grab your spears and lunge toward the man. Your spears enter his body—but he doesn't even flinch! No blood flows from the openings made by the spears.

"He's not human!" you scream.

The white-haired man speaks on, but you don't hear. Your reflexes take over, and you continue to lunge with your spear.

The man's words become slower and more garbled with each thrust. Finally, he stops speaking altogether, and his shell falls shapelessly to the ground.

You stand and stare, awed at what has happened. Just as you realize that you'd better get out of here, you and your friends find yourselves surrounded by a group of robots. They appear bewildered but are quite firm about whisking the three of you off to a small, dark room.

As the door closes behind you, you hear Chark whimper. You feel fear begin to take hold of you, too. Something presses into your leg. You reach down, and your hand feels a familiar shape. It's a bone! You wonder if someone else came to find the reason for the light on Quests Mountain . . . and never went home.

THE END

"I am Ren, and these are my friends, Sars and Chark," you say, wishing your voice wouldn't shake so.

The creature jumps down and stands before you, bow still at the ready. "You have entered gren territory. What business have you here? Speak up!"

"Well, we, uh . . ." We what? You're so nervous you've momentarily forgotten your reason for being here. "Oh, yes! We're on a quest."

"We're trying to discover the cause of the light on the mountaintop," adds Sars.

"Enough!" the green man interrupts. "We do not wish to have dealings with your . . . uh, friends."

For the moment, you ignore the obvious slur to your friends and ask, "We?"

The creature claps his green hands, and suddenly the trees around you are alive with the motions of dozens of other green people.

You're certainly glad you didn't decide to attack!

"Wh—who are you?" Darn your voice!

"We are the gren."

You wonder what Jor would have done in this situation. In your mind, you can hear him saying, "Remember, Ren, the best defense is a good offense." That's it!

"Why do you hide in the trees and pounce on friendly travelers?" you ask, trying hard to keep your voice firm.

The gren seems taken aback by your boldness. "Well . . . they're our trees. We've lived in this glen for as long as our eldest elder can remember."

"We had no intention of harming you or your trees," you say. "YOU'RE the ones who are threatening harm to US."

The gren shuffles his feet nervously. "We've always been rather friendly to your sort, but lately we've been bothered by some creatures, and, well...they've killed some of our people."

"What type of creatures? Were they human of some sort?" you ask.

"No. These creatures seemed to be made of metal," he answers. He pulls you to the side and whispers, "Look, I like your kind, really, and if it weren't for the insistence of my people, I wouldn't have stopped you. But they want me to take some sort of action."

"We ran across one of those robots earlier," you say thoughtfully. "In fact, it saved our lives. Do you know where they come from?"

"I don't wish to talk about them," he says, shaking his head. Then he rushes on. "Listen, perhaps we can help you get to wherever it is you wish to go—unless you wish to see more metal creatures."

"No," you say. "No more metal creatures. We were following a path through the forest when we met the robot, but our real destination is the top of the mountain."

"We can't take you all the way to the mountaintop. There are bad things up there. But we can show you a faster way to the top than following this path."

The gren calls several others over and instructs them to guide you.

Chark slides up to you and whispers, "Do you really think we should go with them?"

"I don't think we have much choice," you whisper back.

Chark glances anxiously at you but follows. Your green guides lead the way.

"How far is this place from here?" your lizard friend asks the guides. They don't answer. Sars looks at you, his eyes snapping with anger.

"Uh, how far is it to this place?" you ask.

"Not far."

You and Sars look at each other and shrug, then walk on in silence.

Soon you reach the top of a steep path. Before you, stretching to the horizon, is the most beautiful view you've ever seen. Nestled between majestic, pine-covered mountains lies a large grove of multicolored trees.

Your guides stop.

"Is this it? How do we get to the top?" Chark asks.

"Journey upward," they answer quickly and promptly leave.

"Wait a moment! Where are we?" you shout after them.

Sars touches your shoulder hesitantly. "Let them go, Ren. They aren't going to help us anymore," he says.

"I'm afraid you're right, Sars. Well, they didn't waste any time," you humph. "And neither should we," you add briskly. "It's getting late. We'd better begin looking for a place to make camp for the night."

You walk along the crest of a hill that slopes gently upward.

"I think I hear water," says Sars. He dashes ahead, stops, and then calls back, "It's a river!"

You discover a faint path through the trees. You follow it until it joins another path that follows the river.

Please turn to page 133.

You know that you probably ought to continue on toward the mountain, but deep down inside, you really want to know where the flying robot is going.

"Let's follow the robot," you say. "It probably won't hurt us."

"Hurry! It's getting away!" Chark hollers over his shoulder as he scurries after the robot.

Fortunately, the course of the robot is so low and so erratic that it cuts a winding path for you to follow through the heavy underbrush.

After some time, Sars says, "We're certainly not heading in a straight line, but we ARE finally moving up the mountain. I've noticed that the vegetation changes with elevation."

"Why can't you just say the plants have changed?" Chark asks irritably. Then he shouts, "Look! A stream!" and dashes ahead.

You hear the sound of rushing water as you follow Chark to a wide, swift stream.

As you pause beside the stream, the robot suddenly bursts through the underbrush up ahead, dips, sputters, rises a bit, then plummets toward the water. There is a loud hissing sound as sparks fill the air, and the robot explodes in a thousand pieces. The three of you dive for cover.

When the shower of metal ends, you gingerly pick up a chunk.

"Ouch!" You quickly drop it and pop your burned fingers into your mouth. You're relieved to discover the burn is not serious.

"Well, now where, Ren?" asks Chark, hands on his hips.

"We follow the stream. It's got to lead to the mountaintop eventually."

Chark and Sars exchange glances, shrug, and follow as you move off upstream.

The sun is halfway down the sky and you have walked a long way through difficult terrain before someone speaks again.

"Do you suppose pieces of that robot could have landed up this far?" asks Sars.

"I doubt it," you say. "Why?"

"Well, I keep seeing metal chunks being swept downstream in the river."

"I don't think they could be from the robot," you say slowly.

"I guess not," says Sars, walking on.

Please turn to page 133.

"Our quest is to reach the top of Quests Mountain and find the cause of the light. We should take the shortest, quickest route." Sars and Chark nod, and you turn toward the west, hoping you have made a good decision.

You come to a narrow path, bordered by thick brush.

It is still early. The sun glows in a vivid blue sky above the Green Lands. "It's been a long time since I've seen a sky that blue," Sars says.

Chark, always eager to hurry, skips ahead of you and Sars.

You watch a moment, then call hesitantly, "Chark, I think you'd better stay closer to us. You know how dangerous the Green Lands are."

You are finding it difficult to start acting like the one in charge. But you must if all three of you are to achieve your quest and return safely.

"I'm all right," Chark grumbles. "You two walk so slow! Let's get going!"

"We want to get there as badly as you do, Chark, but we've got to be careful. This is a dangerous world, and we've got to protect each other."

Chark glances back at you, his feet straying slightly from the path. "Oh, all right," he concedes reluctantly.

Suddenly a blindingly bright light flashes in your eyes. You stand perfectly still, and the light gradually fades. For several moments, all you can see is the lingering image of the white flash.

Momentarily blinded by the light, Chark stumbles off the path once more.

Once again, the light flashes.

"What's going on? Where's that light coming from?" asks Chark.

"Nobody move!" you command.

"Both times the light flashed, Chark had stumbled off the path," Sars says. As his eyes clear, he turns to look at the narrow band of red grass edging the path. "Look at these blackened spots," he continues, pointing with a scaly finger to the ground beside the path.

"Those are my footprints!" gasps Chark.

"Exactly. If anyone steps off the path here, the light flashes," Sars says. "It seems to be nature's way of protecting the forest."

Closing your eyes, you test Sars's theory by stepping off the path onto the grass. Once again the light flashes.

You heave a sigh of relief and begin to walk on, with your friends safely on the path in front of you.

All at once, for no apparent reason, your friends stop and begin to flail their arms about wildly.

"What—what are you doing?" you ask in astonishment. Then you see it: they've walked straight into a huge, gossamer-thin web that stretches across the path. And crashing out of some bushes on the left is a gigantic spider!

You hear a sound behind you. Turning, you

see a metal robot coming down the path straight toward you. As you wonder what to do, a hole opens in the robot's side. A long, thin metal pipe snakes out and sends a jet of green fluid right at you. You dive for cover as the fluid flies over you and hits the spider.

Shaken, you turn to watch as the spider lets out a shriek, curls its hairy limbs close about its body, and drops to the ground in a crumpled heap.

Scrambling to your feet, you turn toward the robot. The pipe has gone back into its body, and the robot is motionless. It almost seems to be waiting for something.

With the danger from that direction apparently past, you turn and rush to your friends and begin hacking at the sticky web with your spear.

"Hurry, Ren," urges Chark. "That robot might decide to come after us."

"I don't think it will." You're not sure why, but you don't think that thing of the Ancients means you any harm.

You finally succeed in freeing your friends from their netlike prison. Chark's hair is matted with bits of the web, and Sars's glasses are gray with the sticky coating.

"Boy, that was close!" Chark exclaims. "If it weren't for that—" He stops suddenly. "What's that written on the front of the robot?"

Sars quickly cleans his glasses and goes over to the robot. Peering intently, he says, "I don't know what this writing means, but I'm going to copy it and study it later. Maybe one of the elders will know." He pulls writing equipment from his pack and scribbles the symbols: ECOLOGY BOT—ORKIN DIVISION.

A shaft of sunlight breaks through the thick trees and falls on the robot. Suddenly it starts to whir, then slowly begins to lift off the ground!

"It's flying!" Chark exclaims. "Let's follow it! Maybe it's going to its home base."

"It seems to be dangerous. Perhaps we should just continue on toward the mountain," Sars suggests.

1) If you wish to follow the robot, turn to page 48.

2) If you think you should continue on toward the mountain, turn to page 102.

"Let's head for the lake," you say. Sars shrugs and begins to walk.

Soon you stand on the shore of a vast lake. In the morning sun, the water looks warm and inviting. You bend over and slowly lower a finger into the water. It's freezing!

"Look! There's something shiny in the water," says Chark.

"Don't touch it!" you warn.

Sars leans over to get a closer look.

"It's metal. It looks like something I've seen in the village a couple of times. But—" he pauses— "this doesn't make sense. It's shiny, and it shouldn't be. It should be rusty from being in the water."

You look around and see more of the shiny chunks of metal in the water and washed up on the shore.

"Something or someone is dumping them here deliberately, or they're being washed into the lake by a mountain stream," you say.

"You remember the robot we saw when we first entered the Green Lands? It was made out of shiny metal. . . ." muses Sars.

"Let's try to find the stream around here that could be carrying this stuff into the lake," you propose.

You begin to walk around the shore of the lake, with Chark skipping on ahead. You soon arrive at a swift mountain stream. Dozens of the metallic chunks swirl in the eddies.

Following the bank upstream isn't as easy as you had anticipated. Rocks, dead branches, and strange, dangerous-looking plants slow you down. Several times, to Chark's dismay, you are forced to step into the icy water to get around them.

"The plant life is getting rather scarce," says Sars after several hours of walking uphill. "And the air seems to be getting thinner."

"My stomach thinks I've forgotten about it," moans Chark, rubbing his belly with the flat of his hand as he plunks down on a low rock.

You stop, accepting the need for a short rest from the hard climb in thin air. You can't even remember when you last ate—your belly has long since ceased its grumblings. But your muscles, raw from a day on the trail and a night on a cave floor, continue to protest.

Chark pulls some food out of his pack and generously offers to share it with you and Sars.

You shake your head. "Save it for yourself. I've still got quite a bit left."

After a few moments, the sweat from your climb has dried on your skin in the chilly mountain air, and you feel very cold and clammy. You bleakly finger your thin tunic, and you realize you must keep moving or slowly freeze. Your muscles complaining at the movement, you stand up again.

"The mountaintop is waiting," you say, pretending an enthusiasm you don't feel. "Let's get going."

"How much farther do you think it is?" asks Chark after a short time.

"It can't be much farther," Sars replies. It isn't much of an answer, but it seems to pacify Chark.

Your bone-weary party moves on in silence.

"It certainly is getting colder." Chark hugs his tunic closer to his hairy body and shivers.

"Just keep moving," you grunt.

Sars comes to a sudden stop. He looks down and announces, "We're getting into the glacial level of the mountain."

"So what does that mean?" spurts Chark impatiently.

"If you'd read your lessons, you'd know that glaciers are huge masses of accumulated snowfall that move like gigantic slow rivers."

"I don't see any big chunks of snow," argues Chark, looking across the expanse of rock and low scrub.

"Even from up close, a glacier doesn't look like snow," says Sars. "It compacts into heavy ice. This whole area should be one big glacier. We're high enough on the mountain."

"The water level back at the lake was pretty high," you say. "And some of the trees near shore were partially underwater. This stream is high for this time of year, too."

"Halt! Where do you think you're going?" rasps a low, gravelly voice. A huge rabbit jumps down from a boulder and lands a few paces in front of you. It's even taller than Sars! Chark turns to run.

"Not so fast!" the creature bellows. It sounds so vicious that you all stop in your tracks.

"Give me something and I won't hurt you," it laughs viciously, rubbing its paws together.

Your mind runs through your scanty provisions, searching for something suitable to give it. Before you come up with anything, you hear a loud BOOM!

The rabbit presses its paws to its floppy ears, jumps straight up in the air, then falls to the ground with a dull thud. To your utter amazement, your tormentor has become a mass of quivering, babbling fur and flesh!

"Oh! They're at it again! Make them stop! No more noise, please!" it cries pathetically. The creature wrings its paws and babbles on, no longer aware of your presence.

You look at the others and see Chark's fear turn to disgust. "Where's the noise coming from?" you ask.

The rabbit ignores you and continues to wring its paws and whimper.

Chark, spear in hand, rushes up to the rabbit. "Oh, quit whining and answer the question!"

The rabbit looks up and swipes one gigantic paw across Chark's spear. The long metal spear bends in half and hangs limp.

"The rabbit turned it to rubber!" wails Chark, hopping backward toward you and Sars.

The evil sneer returns to the rabbit's whiskered face. "Of course I did. And what's more,

there are hundreds like me where I come from.
When I return, I'll tell them to raid your
village."

You turn to look at each other. Is this crazy,
cowardly rabbit telling the truth?

1) If you think the rabbit's telling the
truth, you must go home and warn your
village. Turn to page 123.

2) If you think the rabbit is lying and you
wish to carry on with your quest, turn
to page 129.

"We don't know if the creature's dangerous. She might be friendly. Let's give the cube to her and see what happens," you whisper to your friends. "Go on, Sars. Chark and I will be waiting with our spears, just in case."

"Well, okay," he says, trying to sound confident. Sars takes hesitant steps toward the creature, stopping a good arm's length away. Then he holds out the cube toward the two-headed creature.

The two hands on her right reach out and gingerly take the brightly glowing cube.

"What—I mean, who—are you?" you ask, catching yourself in the nick of time. You don't want to make her angry.

"I am Nel," the right head says sweetly. "And I am Rom," says the left one, mimicking the tone of the first. "We are an orlen," they add, each head nodding to the other in mirrored motion.

"Do you live in this cave?" you ask.

"Yes," they answer in unison. "We love glow cubes," says Nel—or is it Rom?—as they turn it over and over in their clawed hands. "We haven't had one since that group of creatures just like you came to our cave to see those stone creatures in the stream. That was a long time ago. They didn't want to share their cube," the orlen says angrily.

Suddenly you're struck with a marvelous idea. "My friends and I would like you to keep the cube," you say. You hear Sars gasp.

"We're looking for a place to stay for the

night. Where would the safest place be?" you ask.

"Oh, in here, wouldn't you say, Nel?" Nel quickly nods her head. "We were just leaving for dinner when you came—we find the best food at night. You are welcome to stay here."

"Dinner?" asks Chark, licking his brown lips.

"Yes. We've heard that the lemmings are running toward the lake farther up the mountain. Lemmings are quite tasty and many creatures will want them, so we must hurry," says Nel, and the orlen strides toward the door.

"Oh, yes, we must hurry," echoes Rom.

"Tasty, huh? Why don't you bring back one for me?" says Chark, suddenly very chummy.

Nel and Rom turn to say, somewhat haltingly, "Well, they are rather small."

"Then bring me back several," Chark says matter-of-factly.

As the orlen scurries out of the cave, Chark turns to Sars and asks, "What's a lemming?"

"A small, short-tailed, furry rodent," the lizard replies.

Chark gasps and grabs his throat dramatically.

You would have liked to ask the orlen more questions, but you figure that she will return in the morning, so you set about collecting wood for a fire.

"It occurs to me that we don't even know if this cave is safe. How do we know we can trust

the orlen?" Sars asks, adding some dry branches to the pile for the fire.

"Good point," you say. "I guess we were too tired to think of that." Weary as you are, you realize you need to make a decision.

1) If you wish to camp near the entrance to the cave in case you need to get out quickly, turn to page 115.

2) If you would rather explore the cave, turn to page 13.

"Let's get away from here," you decide. "There could be awful things down that hole."

You all rise to your feet, jump on your pinetos, and continue across the desert.

You soon find more rocks that make shade to rest in. Chark, too excited to rest, leans on a boulder and props his head up with his hands to stare out across the desert.

"There's a big, dark arrow shape ahead of us. I can see it flashing in the sun," Chark announces.

You look where Chark is pointing and see through the heat waves given off by the rocks a huge dark shape like a triangle with a tail. "It looks like metal," you say.

"Let's go! It can't be far," Chark says.

With spirits revived by your curiosity, the three of you jump on your pinetos and ride hard. Suddenly you realize that you've been riding a long time, but the thing looks no nearer.

"Chark, we can't keep pushing these mounts. We've got to slow down," you call ahead.

Your monkey friend looks back, disappointed, and reluctantly stops his pineto while you and Sars catch up. Chark's mount looks wilted.

"I don't know why we haven't reached that thing yet," grumbles Sars. "We've been traveling long enough to have gotten there several times over."

"We're tired, and we've used our new mounts too hard," you say, trying to cover your own

disappointment. "Maybe we should rest them, even if there isn't cover around."

As you prepare to dismount, you realize that you're having a difficult time focusing on objects. You look at Sars—his lizard figure shimmers in and out of focus.

Then you realize that the sand below his pineto's feet is also shimmering. Wait! The sand's moving! And what are those strange triangles of rubbery flesh skimming toward you? You squint to steady your vision.

"Land sharks!" you hear Sars scream. Then his cry is abruptly cut off. A fin slices toward you, and your mount is knocked out from under you. Soon you disappear into the harsh reality of the Gamma World.

THE END

"Between our wounds and the darkness," Sars begins, gingerly touching a finger to his arm, "I don't think we should leave this place. The nightwings could find us anywhere—and at least here we have a fire."

"I don't know," says Chark, hesitating. "These rocks didn't turn out to be very safe."

One of your wounds stabs with pain as you move. "Well, we've got to clean these wounds quickly, or they'll become infected," you say. "So we'd better stay here."

"All right. I'll tend to them," Chark volunteers. "Sars first—he looks like he's taken the worst of it."

"I'll get rid of the carcasses," you say. You pick up dead bodies of the nightwings with your spearpoint and toss them far into the darkness beyond the rocks. Then you gather more sticks. Soon the fire is much brighter, but your hopes aren't. You've only just started your quest and all three of you are wounded.

You lay your head back on your pack and slowly drift into a fitful sleep.

Suddenly the noise of thunderously loud wings bursts into your dreams. You open your eyes in time to see a huge black body dive from the sky, pick up Sars in an orange blur, and fly off into the night before you can even make a move.

"It's a yexil!" you cry.

You stare helplessly into the darkness as Sars's shouts for help fade into the distance.

For a moment you see his small, struggling

form outlined in moonlight, but then he's gone.

"What can we do to save him?" Chark asks, grabbing your arm.

"Nothing," you say, hanging your head. "No one's ever escaped from the grasp of a yexil."

Chark jumps up, brushes tears from his hairy cheeks, and stamps his foot. "We HAVE to try SOMETHING! We'll have to search the desert!"

Despite the painful cuts covering his body, Chark turns abruptly and sets out at a run into the desert night.

"Chark! Come back! There's nothing you can do!" you shout after him.

Chark doesn't seem to hear and races across the desert in the direction where you last saw Sars. You shiver as you realize that he'll soon be out of sight.

"I can't lose both my friends!" you think and, summoning all the strength that remains in your wounded body, you run off after Chark.

After several minutes, you see Chark's dim form just ahead. He stumbles over a low bush as you dive for his feet, and you both roll, thrashing, in the sand.

"Do you think Sars would want us to get ourselves killed?" you gasp as you struggle to pin Chark's hairy arms to his body.

Suddenly you feel Chark's body go limp, and he ceases to struggle. "You're right, Ren," he says finally. "There's nothing we can do."

You spend the rest of the night staring into the sky, straining to find an answer—but there is none.

You face the morning with red, sleepless eyes. The thought of never seeing your friend's smiling face is hard to bear. Even if you went on to find the light at the top of the mountain, there would be no joy in it because you have lost one of the best friends you have ever had.

You turn back toward your village, where you'll have to face Sars's parents.

THE END

Hands on hips, you stare up at the metal strip and think about your choices.

You look more closely at the metal strip. The belt itself is about an arm's length wide, with thick metal railings. The whole contraption is held up by thin rods and is suspended straight down from the roof of the tunnel. Once out of the tunnel, it slopes down and around a curve to the right and follows the course of the stream. You begin thinking out loud.

"If this is the same stream we've been following, then this is where—"

"— the metal chunks come from!" finishes Chark.

"The river is so swollen from the melted snow that the belt barely clears it. See? Some of the robots skim the surface of the water and fall off the track and break up in the water. Look," you add. "Those rods holding the track up look mighty shaky. I bet we could pull on the rods and send the whole thing crashing!"

"I don't know. . . ." Chark hesitates.

"This place is the object of our whole quest, and we've got to stop whatever it is that has been going on up here," you say sternly. Another robot slides out above, and you duck out of the way.

Sars shouts, "Look! The robot's covered with ice."

"Ice, smice!" says Chark. "If we're going to break up this operation, let's go!" He waits for the robot to move out of sight, then moves toward the metal belt.

Each of you walks to one of the metal rods. At the count of three, you push against the metal rod with all your might. The rod gives slightly but stays put.

"We'll never be able to budge them!" Chark shouts, slamming his fist against the metal.

You hear a high whining noise. Another robot is coming from the tunnel!

"Hurry!" you urge. All three of you renew your efforts at the supports, trying to rock them loose. The metal belt finally sways, creaks loudly, and then topples into the swiftly flowing river with a loud crash.

You step back just as a new ice-coated robot reaches the broken part of the belt. The robot sails wildly off the belt and hits the water, showering sparks and parts everywhere.

"That ought to fix them!" says Chark, rubbing his hands with satisfaction. "Let's go home!"

Without thinking, you grab his elbow and whirl him about. "Our quest is to see what causes the light," you remind him. He responds with a sheepish look.

You enter the tunnel quickly, ducking down once as another robot roars over your heads. Sars hangs onto your arm as you lead him through the dark tunnel.

Soon you sense that the darkness is changing to a hazy purple hue. You place a hand on your spear and press on toward the light.

The tunnel ends in a small round room, completely enclosed except for the side from which you entered. You stand, puzzled, when suddenly a curved section slides out from the wall and completes the circle. You're trapped!

The ground beneath you shakes and rumbles. A high whining sound fills the air.

"We're going down," says Sars.

As suddenly as it began, the whine slows and turns to a low rumble, then stops with a clank. Ahead of you, a curved wall slides away, revealing a new opening. Your heart is in your throat!

"It's about time you returned. There's been some sort of trouble with conveyor belt Number Four." The speaker is a tall, white-haired, muscular man. His face glows in the light from the equipment below him.

He stands behind a circular counter that comes to his waist. Large, square metal boxes line the sides of the room. From the boxes comes a humming sound. Colored lights blink a staccato pulse from atop each box.

Near the tall man, in the very center of the room, is a piercingly bright stream of purplish light. It comes from a glass, dome-shaped object, passes through three murky, purplish-black stones, and streams onto a small opening in the floor.

"What are you waiting for, A36?" booms the man.

"What's he talking about?" Chark asks nervously.

"He must think one of us is something called A36," Sars whispers. Then he raises his head and says loudly, "I've already corrected the situation, sir."

"What in the world is Sars doing?" mutters Chark.

"Shush!" you say as you watch Sars with growing respect. "That's right, Sars. Keep him talking—maybe you can find out what's going on here. I'm going to check out the rest of this room," you whisper.

"Act as if you belong here," Sars says out of the corner of his mouth.

"Right." Despite your shaking limbs, you straighten your back and stride off toward the side of the room.

Behind you, you hear Sars ask the white-haired man, "What is our next assignment?"

"Master Programmer," says the white-haired man.

Silence. You whirl around and see a blank stare on Sars's face.

"You must call me Master Programmer," the man explains.

Sars sighs, relieved. "Uh, yes, Master Programmer. What is our next assignment?" You can almost feel Sars's relief.

"You must continue your regular duties. The Program will be completed in eighteen hours." With that, your host turns his attention to the equipment before him, obviously finished with Sars.

Suddenly, before Sars realizes what he's doing, Chark asks the man recklessly, "What program?"

The man looks up abruptly and begins to speak in an emotionless voice.

"The Program was devised by the Xenon Corporation in the year 2321 to seize power presently held by the ineffective democratic government.

"Recognizing the current level of worldwide unrest, alliances were formed with sympathetic factions whereby other groups in the alliance are to launch offensive attacks in the form of neutron-based arms.

"Oilcom's role in the Program is to maintain life systems in the major metropolitan centers after the attacks. This complex produces robots immune to radiation, enabling them to maintain systems necessary for relocated human populations."

The man stops his speech and stares down at the table before him.

"What? I didn't understand a word he said about this weird program!" exclaims Chark.

At the word "Program," the man looks up and repeats, "The Program was devised by the Xenon Corporation in the year 2321 to seize power presently held by the ineffective democratic goverment." And he repeats the same speech, word for word.

"Why'd he say the same thing all over again? And what are we going to do now?" Chark asks, obviously confused.

"We're going to continue our regular duties," you hear Sars whisper.

You know the white-haired man can't be

talking about anything in your world, so you begin looking around behind the metal boxes. You find several large, heavy books and open to a page in the first one. You can't understand them, but studying the marks, you see ones you remember seeing before. Teacher Merel had shown you some of the writings of the Ancients. This looks like the same thing! The man must be talking about something of the Ancients!

The man's voice booms over the noise of the machinery: "You are to take your positions at terminals C and D on the left."

Sars and Chark glance at you fearfully, huddle together, and scurry toward the left side of the room.

As they reach the center of the room, Chark unconsciously passes his hand through the purple beam of light.

"My hand!" he screams. You see Sars immediately clasp a hand over the monkey's mouth and hustle him along.

You worry about how badly Chark is hurt, but your attention is caught by the whitehaired man as he speaks again.

"It was foolish of you to touch The Source, A47. You might have endangered the entire Program. Go to Appendage Sector Three and see that your parts are replaced. Then go directly to Conveyor Eight. You have been demoted to the rank of B13."

The Source! You think back over what has happened and realize that, for just a moment, when Chark put his hand in that beam, the noise of the machines stopped. The light must be the source of their energy! Maybe you can do something to stop this fantastic plan.

Trying your hardest to look relaxed, you walk behind the man to the beam. Checking carefully to see that you are not being watched, you place the tip of your spear right in it. You expect the beam to affect the spear somehow, but you are not prepared for what actually happens. The beam seems to bounce off the metal spear and ricochet around the room, momentarily cutting off the power of each machine it contacts.

The lights and noises from the machines keep shutting off and on, off and on.

The white-haired man looks up, the counter opens, and he advances toward you. Your mouth drops open as you see the truth. He is a robot from the waist down!

A yell from Chark snaps you back to attention. "Watch it!" he shouts as the ricocheting beam singes his hairy arm.

Ignoring the half-man, half-robot, you begin trying to control the beam. You turn the spearhead this way and that and soon learn to direct the beam steadily into one row of machines. There is a loud sizzling and sputtering sound as sparks fly from the machines in all directions. Finally the lights atop the machines dim, then fizzle out.

You look up quickly and find that the robot-man is closing in on you. You'll have to do something fast. You also notice robots streaming through a door behind your friends. You hear Sars shout, "Chark, we've got to stop those robots!"

Chark dodges an oncoming robot and grabs a box of metal parts. Stationing himself on the left side of the doorway, he begins tossing parts at the robots. He quickly learns that if he aims at a robot's blinking lights, sparks fly out and the robot stops. Sars catches on and thrusts his spear into the lights, too.

The man stands only an arm's length from you, still talking about the Program. Carefully you angle your spear so that it sends the beam of light into the robot-man's chest. He stops and sways and his words become gibberish.

"The Project . . . go to Appendage Sector Three . . . man your stations . . . eighteen hours . . . Program was devised . . ."

Your arms ache from holding the spear out. The room is now lit only by the purplish glow cast by the beam.

Finally the clanking and whirring noises seem to make a huge sigh as the machines and robots grind to a halt. The high whine from the beam of light is the only sound you hear.

"Well, now what?" asks Chark.

"I don't know," you answer. "If I let the beam return to normal, I'm afraid the robots will start up again."

"Don't do that!" screams Chark.

"I think the source of the beam is those three

stones above us in the dome," says Sars, squinting up at them. "They must be crystals, probably based on the same principle as glow cubes, but much more powerful."

"Then the dome must be the light on Quests Mountain!" you shout, elated.

"I would say so," agrees Sars.

"Do you think we can prevent the robots from ever starting up again by climbing up to the dome and removing the stones?" you ask.

"That should work," says Sars.

"I'll do it!" volunteers Chark, the climber.

"Be careful, Chark! They may be hot," warns Sars.

Chark scampers over to the catwalk on the side of the room, climbs the ladder in three hops, and swings from a beam on the ceiling.

"Quit showing off and get the crystals," you scold sharply.

"Okay, Ren," the monkey says. He pulls himself along the beam hand over hand until he reaches the dome. Licking his finger, he gingerly touches a crystal.

"We're in luck! They're not hot. Here, I'll toss them down." Chark pulls out one of the crystals and drops it into Sars's waiting arms. The room grows dimmer.

"If we remove them all, we won't be able to find our way out," you remind Sars.

"Take only one more out," Sars shouts, a hint of panic in his voice.

You look at your friend closely and say, "Don't worry, Sars. I know that when it's really important, you can overcome your fear of the darkness."

Chark tosses the second crystal down and the room dims even more, but there's still enough light to see by. As he climbs down, he says, "And I guess I've found out that water won't necessarily drown me. But I'd still rather climb than swim any day! Let's go home. I've had it," he adds.

"I'll second that," you answer.

Chark and Sars each take a crystal. You grab Sars's other arm to help guide him through the dark tunnel.

When you emerge, it is dusk. As your weary party begins its climb down Quests Mountain, you know that the village of New Hope won't need to worry about the light on Quests Mountain anymore. And you know one more important thing. From now on, if the situation calls for it, you're not going to worry about being a leader.

THE END

"Let's go back to the start of the Green Lands. We can rest there for the night. I'll guide you, Sars," you say.

"Well, I wanted to go to the mountains anyway," huffs Chark, turning on his heel.

You and Sars smile at each other and follow the hurrying monkey boy.

The moonlight makes eerie shadows of the Great Wastelands as you walk along their southern edge. Chark stops and stares into the land of white ash and bleached bones.

"Why would anything go in there?" he wonders aloud.

You have no answer, so you hustle him along.

You set up camp a short distance from the northwest tip of your village. You look longingly toward home for a moment, then resolutely turn toward the path you'll follow tomorrow.

Taking the first watch, you try to think things out. "I'll have to be more careful. We were lucky, but I should have led more decisively and acted less rashly. I'll make my father proud of me yet." You rest against a boulder, confident that tomorrow will bring you better luck and sharper wits.

Please turn to page 51.

"What do you suppose an 'airplane' is?" asks Chark as you trot away from the huge planting machine.

"We're about to find out," you say.

"Yeah, but how will we know it when we find it?" Chark persists.

"Really, Chark, there isn't that much around here! It shouldn't be too hard to locate," you say, nudging your mount to move faster.

You continue north for some time, staying in sight of the mountains to your left. Gradually the land levels out. The sand is replaced by dry, cracked gray clay. A few gnarled dull-green bushes and tree roots dot the land.

"We've got to rest," you finally say. "It'll do us no good to find this thing of the Ancients if we're too tired to study it. Let's stop and eat something by those rocks ahead on the right."

"Sounds good to me," says Chark, nudging more speed out of his pineto.

You hop from your mount and drop to your knees in a shady area.

"Whew! That sun sure is hot!" you say, wiping your brow. The area around you looks so calm and peaceful that you feel fear and tension leave you.

You lean back, resting your head on an old log. You close your eyes ... and fall backward! Jerking into a sitting position, you turn and see that the ground around the log has collapsed into a huge hole. Your heart leaps into your throat as you realize how easily you could have gone in, too.

"It must be the opening to something's den—and I bet it's nothing nice," Chark whispers.

"Notice that it's not dark down there. Something must be giving off light," Sars says.

"Notice that something very, very big must have made that hole!" Chark shouts.

"We must investigate," says Sars.

"We have to get away from here," insists Chark. "I have a bad feeling about that hole, and I certainly don't want to climb down into it."

1) If your curiosity is greater than your fear, turn to page 89.

2) If you'd rather play it safe, ignore the hole, and continue on toward the airplane, turn to page 65.

You continue walking in silence. Soon you top a tall pile of rocks where you can see what lies ahead. About thirty paces in front of you is a large, gray stone cliff. In the face of the cliff are three large, round openings. A narrow path runs across the front of the cliff face. To the right of the cliff is a stream.

"I think we've finally made it to the top," Chark says softly.

"Well, let's go see what's in those openings," you say.

You walk to the opening on the left. It's dark inside, so you step in a bit farther. You feel hot air and hear loud noises somewhere in the distance.

You leave the tunnel and go to the center opening. In contrast, this tunnel is blindingly bright. When you step inside, you feel cold air and notice an almost eerie silence.

Going over to the opening on the right, you see a moving belt of some sort mounted on the cavern ceiling. The belt continues on out the opening above the stream.

As you are pondering what it might be, you hear a clanking and whirring noise. You duck just in time to avoid being hit by something whizzing past on the belt and out the opening. It's a metal robot! It rounds a corner of the belt and sails out above the stream.

You stand up, dust yourself off, and say, "Strange! I have a feeling that the light comes from up here somewhere. We're going to have to investigate these openings."

"Yeah, but which one?" asks Chark.

You think for a moment before speaking. "If we go into the hot, dark opening, we'll have several advantages. If anything's in there, it won't be able to hear us coming over the noise. And something has to be making that noise. Of course, we won't be able see in the dark, and we'd have to lead Sars.

"If we go into the cold, bright cave, at least we'll be able to see, but so will anything that's in there.

"And if we enter the third opening, the one the robot shot out from, we'll be able to investigate that."

You dive to the ground as another robot shoots out of the opening and down the metal belt.

Which entrance will you enter?

1) If you think you should enter the dark, hot opening where the noises are coming from, turn to page 40.

2) If you think the bright, cold opening offers a better chance, turn to page 97.

3) If you want to enter the opening that the robots are coming from, turn to page 72.

You don't even get to announce your decision. Sars says firmly, "The hole is just too interesting to pass up," and he drops down without glancing to see if you're both following him.

"I'm usually the one who rushes in," says Chark, sighing.

"Sars sure hasn't left us much choice. Well, let's get in there and make sure he doesn't get hurt," you say. You plunge into the hole behind Sars and find yourself in a lighted tunnel.

You look closely at the glassy smooth walls and realize that the light comes from a glowing moss that grows on them. The moss-light lets you see a long way ahead.

"It's wonderful!" Sars says, more to himself than to you. "I wonder what type of creatures could build such a home?"

Sars gets his answer as the corridor widens into a large room.

Ants! The room is filled with huge ants! Each one must be longer than Sars is tall.

A few of the giant insects notice you but go on nibbling on a giant leaf.

"How remarkable!" Sars says. "This species has grown to a huge size and is greatly different from the ants at home."

"I didn't like ants there," says Chark, "and I like them even less here! Let's get out of here fast!"

"Oh, we don't have anything to worry about—these are worker ants," Sars says.

"However, we probably should watch out for their larger fighter types. . . ."

"Larger than THAT?" says Chark, aghast.

"Oh, yes. Considerably larger, I should think. The warrior ants would probably fill up these tunnels with their bodies. Notice how much larger the tunnels are than they need to be for the workers. Ants don't do work they don't have to do."

You feel a rush of air behind you and look back into the tunnel you've just left. The opening is filled by a gigantic ant sweeping toward you, its feelers waving frantically!

"It's a warrior ant!" says Sars. "Smell that odor. Ants often communicate through odors. It's probably warning the nest about intru—"

Sars stops abruptly, exclaiming, "WE'RE the intruders! We've got to get out of here!"

"What do you suggest, brain? The tunnel is blocked!" says Chark angrily.

"Just run!" you shout.

You trip over each other as you find and stumble into a passage to your left. The warrior ant is close behind you.

You speed up and burst out of the tunnel into the open. You stop abruptly as you realize that you're on a ledge high on the wall of a giant cavern.

You stare down into a huge room lit entirely by moss plants. The floor of the cavern is a vast expanse of delicate structures shaped like beautiful crystal buildings.

Far across the room, some worker ants seem

to be spitting out a white liquid that hardens into the beautiful crystal shapes. You watch as an ant puts the finishing touches on a lacy spire.

The spectacle of the strange ant city takes your breath away. Even with danger behind you, you pause in wonder at the sight.

But then you remember your peril. "We've got to move!" you say, hurrying the others along the ledge that encircles the upper level of the cavern city.

You pass several tunnels opening off the ledge before you look behind and find that more monster ants have joined the chase. Looking ahead, you realize that still more of them are on the ledge in front of you.

Your path is blocked! Quickly you glance into the two tunnels nearest you. One is dark and silent. The other is lit by the strange moss, and you think you hear the sound of running water somewhere inside.

Which tunnel will you enter?

1) If you choose to escape down the dark tunnel, turn to page 141.

2) If you'd rather take a chance on the dimly lit tunnel with the running water, turn to page 125.

"Run, Chark!" you shout. "There are too many of them for us to fight!" The monkey boy snaps to attention and barely manages to turn his pineto just before a dog-man swings at his legs.

You dig your heels into your own mount and move swiftly across the dune and away from the dog-men.

Looking back, you see that the dog-men show no sign of stopping their pursuit. The pinetos must sense your fear because they move faster than you would have thought a plant could ever move. You thank the luck that took you to them. Without your plant mount, you would surely have been caught by now!

You start to breathe a little easier as the distance between you and the dog-men widens, though they continue the chase.

Soon you again reach the metal machine, still digging up sand. You hide behind it on the side away from the dog-men. The thing suddenly stops digging. In some way you feel it become aware of the dog-men, a greater threat to it than you and your friends are.

The machine stirs, and you hear it shout over the noise of the dogs in the language of your people!

"More arks to bother my gardens? Well, I know how to take care of you pests. No dog is going to mess up my plantings!" Several huge, moving saws emerge from its side, angled toward the dogs.

The barking soon turns to howls. Those dog-men who aren't hurt by the blades run for their lives.

Lame blows from the dog-men's clubs have dirtied the machine a bit, but haven't even dented it. The machine runs its blades through the sand once to clean them off and puts them back wherever they came from.

You and your friends sit on your mounts watching with astonishment. As the last dog-man yelps out of sight, the machine turns to you.

Please turn to page 116.

"The water will have to wait, Sars. I think I have enough to share with you," you say. "We're heading for the airplane."

Soon you see in the distance a huge arrow-shaped thing making a dark shadow on the sand.

"Do you suppose that's the airplane thing?" asks Chark, eagerness in his voice.

"Just watch, Ren. He's going to want to climb it," says Sars.

"Well, why not?" demands the monkey boy, anger in his voice.

"Let's race," you interrupt. "We're almost there!"

Your friends look a little ashamed of how close they were to arguing, and they spur their mounts to move faster. You race across the sand until you reach the strange shape that rises out of the rocks.

It isn't until you reach the huge object that you realize it is made of metal.

"It must be the airplane of the Ancients!" you say, awe in your voice.

"Didn't the Ancients build anything small?" Chark asks.

"Our whole village could live in one small section," says Sars.

"I wonder how we get in?" you ask, trying to sound practical. "It would be foolish to go back without having tried."

"It has been around since the time of the Ancients and must be filled with valuable secrets about the past. We could take them back to our village with us," Sars suggests.

You ride around the huge thing and find only two openings. Both are on the same side. One is at ground level, and it's smooth and oblong. Much higher up is another, with an irregular shape and jagged edges.

1) If you choose to enter the lower opening, turn to page 34.

2) If you'd rather climb the side of the airplane and go through the top opening, turn to page 153.

"We're going into the center opening, where it's bright, so we don't have to guide Sars," you say. "Then we'll all have our hands free in case something happens."

You lead the way along the path to the opening in the center and step into a different world. The tunnel walls are thick with ice glistening in the light. It is deathly silent.

"Boy, it sure is bright in here!" You duck instinctively as your words bounce off the ice walls and echo in your ears.

"Wow," Chark breathes softly. "Some place!"

"If it gets any brighter, I don't think we're going to be able to follow it to the end," you whisper, and the tunnel mimics back, *"end... end ... end."*

"I believe we're heading downward," says Sars. "At least there seems to be some slope."

"It's slippery, too," you add.

"I'm beginning to think we might actually be inside a glacier," says Sars.

The glare of the bright light on the ice almost blinds you now.

"We're going back," you say. Chark promptly turns, loses his footing, and falls. You pick him up by the arm.

"I think I've made a bad choice," you confess.

"We're going to have a difficult time getting back up. This slope is much greater than it seemed," says Sars, turning to start back.

Anxious to get out of the icy tunnel, Chark leaps ahead of you and Sars. You see a whirl of feet and arms as he slips once more on the icy tunnel floor and goes sprawling with a yelp. He struggles to stand, but the floor of the tunnel is so slick that he can't get up. He begins to slide toward you with alarming speed.

"Help!" he howls.

You reach out, hoping to stop his slide, but the ice has him now, and the momentum of his slide pulls you with him!

You scramble for footing but make no headway. As you slide faster and faster, the light of the tunnel becomes brighter and brighter. Finally the pain to your eyes from the light becomes too great. You close your eyes, but the light still sears through.

Legs numb from the cold, eyes blinded by the light, you cease struggling and resign yourself to your endless slide.

THE END

You all gallop around the oasis a few times to get used to your mounts. Riding on the back of a spiny plant is very strange indeed, but it's a lot better than walking. You feel as though you should say things to your pineto, but the plant only responds to the controls on its headstalk.

"Let's head northwest, away from the sun and toward the mountain, at least until noon," you say. "We can always turn back if we don't like what we see."

You ride off, laughing and joking despite your tiredness.

Sars is the first to spot the fountain of sand

"What's that?" he asks, pointing into the distance.

"Let's move closer. With our pinetos, we can surely get away quickly if we need to," you suggest.

You nudge your mounts slowly toward the stream of sand and stop twenty or so paces from the source. From that distance you can see that a huge metal machine—probably a thing of the Ancients, you decide—scoops out hole after hole in the sand. But each scoopful streams out of the container and falls back, filling the holes in again.

"Teacher Merel told us that machines like these were often intelligent," says Sars. "Maybe we should talk to it."

"They were also pretty dangerous," comments Chark. "I think we should ride around it. We can always come back to it. At the rate that it's making holes, it's not likely to go anywhere."

Both of them turn to look at you for a decision.

1) Will you go around it and avoid facing a possibly dangerous—but possibly helpful—metal monster? Turn to page 120.

2) Or will you talk to the metal creature and see if you can learn things about the desert? Turn to page 116.

You draw a deep breath and say, "Let's continue on up the mountain. The robot seems to be in bad condition and will probably only lead us on a fruitless chase."

As you go, you are careful to stay on the natural path that seems to angle up toward the mountaintop.

"I'm glad we decided to go through the Green Lands, even after the spider and the strange robot," says Chark.

"I don't understand why they call this area the Green Lands, though," says Sars. "Just look at all the colors." Almost every color of the rainbow seems present in the trees and bushes that dot the landscape. Every now and then, a bright beam of sunlight breaks through the treetops and brightens the forest floor with a breathtaking hue of colors.

"Even the rocks are colored," Sars adds. He picks up several small rocks and juggles them for a moment. Then they drop to the ground in a symphony of bell-like musical tones.

Startled, Sars bends quickly to investigate and trips over another rock at his feet. Much to his surprise, it honks sweetly at him.

You smile and draw deeply of the fresh mountain air. Chark skips on ahead, while Sars continues to inspect almost everything that catches his eye.

"Halt and identify yourselves!"

Startled, you look up the path but see nothing. Chark and Sars stare at you, looking as puzzled as you feel.

"Yes, you! Up here!" the voice continues. You look up. Perched high on a tree branch above the path is a totally green man!

"You will not speak, then? I'm sure that, with a little coaxing, you and your lizard and monkey friends will have something to say," he says with a sneer. The green man shifts slightly, giving you a view of the bow and arrow in his green hand.

"I knew it! I knew things were too peaceful!" whispers Chark.

You must act fast.

1) Should you talk to this strange green creature? Turn to page 44.

2) Do you want to run and hope that you can get away from it? Turn to page 36.

3) Or do you want to try to attack the creature and kill it? Turn to page 112.

The oasis is a stunning contrast to the sandy desert dunes. There are splashes of color everywhere. Plants burst with shockingly bright multicolored blooms. There are striped and polka-dotted trees, bushes in every design imaginable.

The beauty does nothing to hide the danger of each plant. Each is spiked or jagged or conceals bulbs of poison just waiting for the unwary to touch them. Not even the impetuous Chark dares look closely.

"Why are we bothering to look at all of these plants anyway? None of them looks good to eat," says Chark. "We could be riding our pinetos! I think I'll name mine Daywind—after the area where we found it."

"You could call it Dead Duck—after its careless master, if you walk much closer to that shooting cactus," Sars says, quickly throwing a dead branch at a large, thorny, ball-like plant. A blinding white light flashes from the center and burns the branch to a cinder.

"What was that?" yells Chark.

"If you had studied more, you would have known to be careful of that plant. There are several others here that will do the same if you don't watch out," warns Sars. Red-faced, Chark looks down at his feet.

"We must find a safe place to rest," you remind them.

Your friends soon forget their anger.

Finding nothing immediately dangerous, you soon announce, "We should be fine here for the day. But I bet there are strange things that come here to drink at night. We better leave at sunset.

"You two go ahead and rest while I stand the first watch."

"Okay, but if anything happens, you be sure and wake us up," says Chark, yawning.

As your friends sleep, you explore further. You can't go too far away—your friends are counting on you to protect them.

Walking space in the oasis is cramped. Some plants you recognize as being dangerous, so you avoid them, but to be safe, you must also not touch the plants you don't know.

One patch of flowers in particular catches your eye. You bend over and look at one yellow bloom more closely. The blossom grows from a bulblike stem and has five thick, wavy, bright yellow petals that look like the fingers of a hand.

Curious but cautious, you stand to one side and use your spear to poke the blossom. No dangerous seeds or rays shoot out, but a gooey yellow sap oozes from the wound.

When you bend to touch the fluid, a searing pain shoots through your head, throwing you to the ground. Through growing darkness you hear a voice.

"Human, you have thoughtlessly killed some of our number. Your race has always been thoughtless." The voice bypasses your ears and speaks directly to your mind.

"Who are you? What are you?" you ask as if in a dream.

"We are the Collectors of Light. Your ancestors indirectly created us in their great struggle many passings of the sun ago. Because of the debt that we owe your race for our beginnings, we will give you the gift of understanding. Watch and learn."

You see yourself among the yellow flowers, which you know are the Collectors of Light.

Then the vision shifts, and you are looking across the desert beyond the oasis. But in the blink of an eye, the desert changes to a cool scene of green fields filled with sweet plants. The plants are tended by metal creatures that you recognize as belonging to the Ancients. You travel over these fields to a huge village inhabited by the Ancients. They look just like the pure strain humans of your village!

"You could live like this again," says the voice in your dreams.

Then you see huge arrows of metal flying toward the dream village. The arrows explode, and immense fires of unimaginable force destroy the village in an instant. All the people die at once. But the destruction doesn't stop there — the land is burned, animals of all types and sizes die, or if they survive, their offspring are horribly mutated by an invisible force given off by the exploding arrows.

"This is how it started. You will see how it could end," the voice breaks in again.

The dream blurs, and you find yourself

above your own village of New Hope. You see the homes of your friends. Your own mother and father stand by the river.

Suddenly the forest around the village parts, and hundreds of metal monsters of the Ancients move through your town, destroying everything that gets in their way.

Your father moves toward one with his weapons and is knocked to the ground.

"Father, run!" you shout.

The image fades and you hear the voice again. *"This is the future that might happen. You must see that it does not."*

"How can I do that?" you ask.

"Go to the Mountain of Light and end what has begun there—or we all will be doomed."

You feel the voice begin to pull and shake you. But when you open your eyes, you see Sars's bespectacled face.

"Ren! Are you all right?"

"We pulled you out of those plants," says Chark. "What were you doing in there?"

All that you have just seen is but a wisp of dream slipping away from your memory. But you cannot forget the scene of your father being attacked by that metal thing.

"We have to go on to the mountain," you tell your friends. "I'm not sure why, or even how, but we must reach the light on the top of Quests Mountain."

"No problem," says Chark. "Right, Sars?"

Sars hesitates, then nods.

"We slept all night, Ren. We were lucky

nothing attacked us." Sars grins, pointedly not mentioning that you, too, slept.

"I'm truly sorry about that. We could have been killed because of me." You hang your head for a moment and then rise briskly.

"Let's get going. The sooner we reach the mountains, the better I'll feel."

You quickly swallow some water and dried food before leaving the oasis.

"The only thing better than a good pineto is a tree with a lot of branches to climb," comments Chark. "I don't know why we don't have these at home."

"Pinetos can't stand the moisture of our land and would quickly rot away," says Sars. "We will have to let them go when we reach the mountain."

"No way!" yells Chark.

"Chark, we're going to have to climb cliffs to reach the mountaintop from this side. Can you imagine these poor things trying to climb a cliff?" you ask.

"Oh," Chark says sadly. "I never thought of that. Why are you always right, Ren?"

"I wish I were," you say, laughing. "Don't worry. We can always come back and find more pinetos. Remember, after this adventure we'll be adults."

"I hardly think that's —" Sars starts to say but is interrupted by Chark.

"That'll be great. I'm going to capture lots of these and sell them. You two will help me, of course. It'll be fun!"

You both sigh, knowing Chark will never change—and neither of you wants him to.

You reach the cliffs safely and prepare to say good-bye to your faithful pinetos. Chark's eyes well with tears. He looks away from you quickly, hugs his pineto, unleashes its lead, and lets it go free.

No one speaks for a few moments as you and Sars do the same with your pinetos.

Chark swallows hard and looks upward. "The climb doesn't look too difficult, but it's a long way. Good thing we have rope."

"We'll have to work fast to get up there before the sun goes down," says Sars.

"This is going to be tougher than I thought," you say, looking straight up the cliff face before you.

"No, it won't. Climbing is easy!" brags Chark, ignoring his rope and bounding up the rocky cliff. His nimble fingers and toes find holds where you can't even see them.

You and Sars follow, using rope. Soon, even Chark has a hard time finding handholds. But the monkey boy would never admit it.

"I told you this would be easy—and fun!" Chark says gleefully.

As Chark smiles down at you, the rock in his right hand breaks loose from the cliff. He scrambles frantically to find something to grab—but there is nothing.

"Chark!" you scream.

As Chark plummets toward you, Sars whips out his powerful tail and bats the thin, airborne monkey like a ball. When Chark hits the cliff next to you, you grab him quickly, holding him until he finds a handhold.

No one speaks as Chark, the wind knocked out of his body, gulps air into his lungs.

"Thanks, Sars," he gasps after some time. The lizard shrugs but looks pleased.

The rest of the climb passes quietly and quickly. Chark moves much more carefully.

Just when you think your arms and legs can climb no more, you reach the top of the cliff face. Pulling yourself up onto a ledge, you see in dismay that more mountain stretches ahead of you.

"Where's the light?" Chark asks.

"Well, we're certainly not at the top yet." You look around and then point up the mountain. "It looks as if there's a lake up there." You see blue water sparkling through the trees in the late afternoon sun.

"And I bet there's a stream feeding the lake from the top of the mountain. We ought to be able to follow it up," you say. "But let's rest for the night right here. I don't think I can walk one more step."

You awaken in the morning refreshed and relaxed.

Please turn to page 56.

You pull Chark close and whisper, "Climb up the tree and attack. Sars and I will throw rocks to keep him busy while you move up with your spear."

Chark hesitates, nods agreement, and scampers off.

You search the ground for rocks, but before you can throw the first one, the trees around you seem to come alive—from every branch appear more of the green creatures! They drop to the ground and surround you before Chark has even begun to climb.

Three of them grab your arms. You twist to free yourself, and in your struggles, you trip over the foot of one of your captors. Searing pain shoots through your head as it meets a rock embedded in the forest floor. The trees around you darken, and the last you remember is the sight of swarms of the green creatures surrounding your friends.

You awaken to thoughts of green men dancing wildly about you and sit up abruptly. You close your eyes and try to clear your head. Then, spitting dirt and sand from your mouth, you open your eyes to look for your friends. You discover them sitting a short distance away, looking groggy. A chill runs down your spine and you look down at your body.

"My clothes are gone! And so is my gear! They've taken everything!" You mourn the loss of your precious spear even more than your clothes.

"Mine, too!" wails Sars.

"What do we do now?" asks Chark.

You try to think, then say sadly, "We must go back to the village."

"Go back now? Without even the clothes on our backs? We'll be laughingstocks!" Chark explodes.

"It could be worse you know," says Sars. "We're still alive."

"If they had killed us, at least we wouldn't have to go back to the village naked," complains Chark.

"We'll just have to try to stay warm the rest of the night, then set off for the village in the morning."

As you huddle by your friends, trying to keep warm, stones and branches on the forest floor scratch your aching body. Your mind turns to thoughts of your brother Jor. At least he won't have to see you return to your village of New Hope in utter disgrace.

THE END

You huddle together near the entrance of the cave. You decide not to build a fire because it might attract strange creatures. Fortunately, the mountain air on this night is warm. It has been a busy day, and some food and a soft skin to lie on soon put you to sleep.

You awaken shortly before sunrise. Groggily, you rouse Sars and Chark from their slumber.

"Wake up, you guys. Maybe we should leave before the orlen returns," you suggest.

"Yes!" Chark nods vigorously, grateful for a way to avoid facing his lemming problem.

"Let's head toward the lake the orlen mentioned," says Chark. "She — THEY — said it was farther up the mountain, so it won't be out of our way." He climbs a tall tree and spots a body of water in the distance.

Within half an hour, you come to a ridge overlooking the lake. The path continues along the ridge.

"Maybe we should just go on up the mountain," Sars suggests. "We're almost there."

"Yes, but how do we know that going to the lake won't be a shortcut?" asks Chark.

What do YOU think?

1) If you wish to continue on toward the lake, turn to page 56.

2) If you'd rather continue straight up the mountaintop, turn to page 87.

"I believe it wants to talk to us," says Sars.

"Yeah, but what do you say to something like this? It's rumored that many of the machines of the Ancients were more intelligent than the Ancients themselves," you say.

"Ask it what it's doing here," proposes Sars.

Chark boldly jumps off his mount and addresses the creature. "Metal Monster, what are you doing here in the desert?"

"Very tactful, Chark," you moan, rolling your eyes. You prepare to defend yourself against an offended creature.

Instead, the creature speaks to Chark in the wobbly voice of a friendly old man.

"Well, now my sensors have seen everything," it says "Who would have calculated that a mutant species could develop verbal communication patterns? Do you have any other useful programs, mutant?"

"I don't know what you mean, machine, but I have been found useful in certain places. What's it to you?" Chark asks with narrowed eyes.

You hastily add, "We're new to these lands and were wondering what you're doing here."

"Well, a pure strain human!" It sighs with pleasure. "I have been programmed to plant tropical foliage in this part of the country. Funny . . . I used to be able to drop a seed anywhere around here and it would grow— but that was a long time ago. Any unit can see that planting here now is a useless undertaking, but my programming remains intact. Is

there anything else I should be doing?" it asks you.

You don't know what to say. It's as if the thing wants you to command it.

"I'm sure you're doing a fine job," you say kindly. "Tell me—do you know anything about these lands?"

It heaves a huge, echoing sigh and slowly begins digging again while it talks.

"To the north, right along the mountain ridge, is an airplane—it looks to be in good shape, too, from what I can tell."

The creature pulls out a wet fern plant in little shovel-like hands, drops it into an already sand-filled hole, pours water on it from a small metal container on its side, and pats the sand down.

"To the southeast is a large oasis that I made—did rather a nice job if I do say so myself. Let's see . . . something that will last in this sandbox."

The metal creature begins to dig two more holes, which fill with sand before it can finish. "Beyond that, high in the mountains, is a robotic installation. It sends me signals now and again." Then it adds thoughtfully, "Just started doing that a little while ago.

"About the only other thing you're going to find is sand . . . and more sand." It drops another plant into another filled hole.

"You know, my job would be much easier if all types of desert pests would stop charging me. I have had to go on vermin watch nearly every day this week. It really saps the reserves of a poor ecology bot, if you know what I mean."

You don't, but you say you understand. Then you thank the machine and bid it farewell.

You gallop a short distance away from the machine before speaking.

"We've already seen the oasis, but it says this 'airplane'—whatever that is—is right along the mountain ridge."

"I'd certainly like to see that!" says Sars.

"I'd rather climb the mountain," says Chark. "After all, that's where we're supposed to be headed."

1) If you wish to go back to the oasis to rest and then on to the mountaintop and its "robotic installation," turn to page 131.

2) If you'd rather take time to find out what an airplane is, turn to page 85.

"We've got to go around," you say. "Things of the Ancients are dangerous, and you can never tell which way they will jump. Let's hold to our plan and travel until noon."

The sand dunes rise and fall under your new mounts. Each dune looks like the last, and they stretch on endlessly. Occasionally, a larger dune breaks the dullness.

You reach the crest of yet another dune, stop your mount, and turn in your saddle to wait for your friends. Sars rides up next to you and pulls back on the reins of his pineto.

"I must admit that even I don't find much to study in this dry country. Sand looks like sand. I suppose the ripples made by the wind are kind of interesting, but . . . have you noticed that there are no ripples in that stretch of sand before us? I wonder why," mutters Sars.

"Who cares? It's only one more patch of useless sand we have to cross," says Chark. "We might as well get going. It's not doing us any good to sit up here in the hot sun," he says crossly.

"Wait, Chark! I don't like the looks of that sand, either," you say.

Suddenly your eye is caught by movement. Huge, doglike men appear from nowhere and charge up the hill toward you, barking fiercely. They carry large wooden shields with strange symbols on them and wave heavy stone clubs at you as they stream up the hill.

You turn your mount to run but notice

Chark out of the corner of your eye. He is frozen in place, watching in horror as the two-legged dogs run toward him. The dog-men will be on you in moments! You must run immediately or fight!

1) If you want to run, taking the chance that Chark might not be able to get away, turn to page 93.

2) If you decide that the best defense is a good offense, charge down the hill at them and turn to page 140.

"I don't think we'd better take any chances. Grab it!" you whisper.

Chark and Sars rush over to the startled rabbit and haul it up off the ground. You pull a length of rope from your pack and tie its paws behind its back.

"You're coming with us, rabbit," you say.

It holds its furry chin high and says, "You know, if I don't return soon, my people will come looking for me. And by the way, you can call me Larry," it adds.

"We'll be far away by then, and your people won't know which way we went," says Chark, pushing Larry along.

The rabbit nods its head and wrinkles its chin. "Good point," it concedes.

You march Larry past the lake. "Do you know where those metal chunks in the lake come from?" you ask.

"Of course I do," Larry says smugly. "But I'm not telling."

In anger, you raise your spear, then notice too late that the rabbit's paws are loose. It sweeps one furry paw across your spear and instantly the weapon goes limp in your hands. Larry smiles at you sweetly.

"That does it!" you shout. You rush toward the rabbit, reaching for its throat. It merely laughs, jumps over your head, and hops back up the path, the length of rope still dangling from one paw.

Chark tries to go after it, but Larry hops too fast. Far up the path, it turns to face you.

"Sorry, folks, but good old Larry lied. I'm the last of my kind around these parts. Some tribe of hoops, eh? Oh, what fun!" The rabbit laughs, claps its paws gleefully, then pounds its chest proudly.

"Come back when you want to play again," it shouts, and it hops out of sight.

"That's just great! We get tricked by a screwy rabbit," Chark says, stomping his foot into the dirt.

Sars stands by, holding the only useful spear left. "We can't possibly expect to make it to the top of the mountain with one spear, especially if we can be tricked so easily."

You nod slowly, squint toward the mountaintop—so close but now so inaccessible —and head back down the mountain.

THE END

Remembering Sars's fear of darkness, you rush headlong into the lit tunnel. It immediately opens up into two caverns, one on each side of the passage. Both caverns are filled with neatly stacked boxes. If only you knew what was in them! Maybe it's something of the Ancients!

Then you spot a river flowing between the stacks of boxes, into the darkness beyond.

Quickly choosing between the giant ants or the water—not much of a choice as far as you're concerned—you shout, "We've got to jump!"

You grab one of Chark's arms while Sars grabs the other, giving him no time to think, and you all jump into the waters below.

A swift current grips you and sends you careening, but you manage to keep afloat. Your legs and arms scrape against underwater rocks, but you are swept away before you can catch hold of anything.

Suddenly you feel yourself thrust out of the water, and you struggle to remain on the surface. Opening your eyes, you find yourself in a pool, being pounded by the spray of an underground waterfall!

Looking frantically around for Chark, you find him clinging to a nearby rock, the fear slowly fading from his face. Then you realize that you can see him because more of the glowing moss lines the cave walls.

"What's this?" asks Sars, fingering a chunk of metal floating by him.

Swirling in the water around you are countless more bits of curved metal, which appear to have been broken off something. You see that some of the chunks have washed up onto the sandy beaches surrounding the lake.

As you make your way to shore, you say, "I wonder where these things come from."

"Wherever the stream that feeds this lake comes from," answers Sars.

"Thanks," you say sarcastically. "And where might that be?"

"Well, this stream comes from the mountains," Sars replies matter-of-factly.

"How in the world do you know that?" Chark asks, his curiosity reviving after finding himself in water and still alive.

"The water is cold—much colder than this cavern. So the lake must be fed by a mountain stream, maybe from a glacier."

"And if we find the stream, we find a way out!" you shout with joy.

"It shouldn't be too difficult to find," Sars adds.

Emerging from the water, you and your friends separate to look for the stream. You soon find a gently flowing, shallow stream coming from a high tunnel.

You turn to tell your friends but spot Chark among the metal rubble on the beach. He's holding a fist-sized oblong object with a small ring on the top. You remember your uncle telling you about such a thing—that it was very dangerous!

"Chark, throw that thing away! It's going to explode!" You watch the monkey hurriedly toss the thing far over his shoulder, then you dive at Sars. Knocking his large form to the ground, you throw yourself on top of him as a massive explosion rocks the cavern.

You open your eyes to see sun filtering through the dust and falling dirt.

"Uh, I found the way out, guys," Chark says sheepishly, sitting up.

"Are you crazy?" you and Sars say at the same time.

Chark—in his element again—leads the way up through the opening carved out by the explosion to solid ground.

"I hope our pinetos are still here," calls Chark as he races ahead of you.

You find your plant steeds a little wilted but otherwise unharmed. Chark skips up to his and gives it a hug.

"We need rest, but—" You glance down at the hole that started it all. "I'd rather not be ant food. Let's ride away and look for someplace else to rest."

You all get flasks of water out of your packs, give some to your pinetos, and set off across the desert. Soon you find another group of boulders and scout the area. Finding it safe, you camp there for the night.

In the morning, you return to the oasis, planning to head for the mountaintop.

Please turn to page 104.

"The rabbit's lying," says Chark. "Let's move on."

"My name is Larry," the rabbit says testily. "We'll just see who's lying."

"Just in case, we're taking you with us," you say, looking at Larry through narrowed eyes. Chark and Sars move toward the creature, but Larry leaps high into the air and lands on a boulder above you.

"The monkey's right. I was lying, but at least I got away, didn't I?" it sneers and hops out of sight among the boulders.

"Well, at least we're rid of it," you say. Then you notice Chark looking sadly at his rubber spear. "Don't worry, Chark. We've got two more."

"That's just great," he says. "I'm going to keep my eyes open for that rabbit when we come back down the mountain."

You turn around and continue up the path. You notice Sars bending over to look at something.

"What is it, Sars?"

"I'm still puzzled about the glacier," Sars says slowly. You can tell from the scratches on the rocks that there was once a glacier here. But the climate hasn't changed, so it should still be here."

Please turn to page 87.

"The mountain is our primary objective. The sooner we get there, the faster we solve the mystery of the light, but let's rest at the oasis first before moving on," you say.

"Good! We've already wasted a lot of time," says Chark.

"No time is wasted when you learn something," says Sars sternly.

You and Chark look at each other and exchange smiles.

In the welcome coolness of the oasis, you quickly tie the pinetos to some trees and move to the pool. Your feet in the water, you lean your head back on a pillow of grass. Just as you start to fall asleep, you hear a soft hissing or grating sound. You lift your head, look around, and finding nothing, relax again.

The hissing noise returns, louder than ever. With your head pressed to the ground, you realize that something's moving underneath you!

"Climb a tree!" you shout as you jump to your feet.

"Wha . . . huh?" Sars sits up, confused.

"Just get up a tree!" You push your friends toward the nearest one.

Sitting on a branch in the tree with Chark and Sars glaring at you, you begin to feel a bit foolish.

Sars looks longingly at the ground where you were just resting peacefully. "Look at that!" he suddenly yells, pointing toward the pinetos.

You see a strange, rubbery-looking black triangle cutting through the sand toward your mounts. Then you spot several more moving in the same direction.

Before the poor plants even sense danger, they are surrounded by large, gray fishlike creatures that leap out of the sand as if it were water. The creatures tear at the pinetos with sharp, savage teeth, giving them no chance to escape.

"Land sharks!" exclaims Chark, his monkey face pale. "That could have been us!"

"Let's move on," you say. "I think we can make the high ridge line of the mountain by late afternoon."

Please turn to page 87.

The path suddenly opens into a clearing, and you realize that the river now flows between high walls.

"Those walls have been built by someone," observes Sars.

"How str—" You are stopped in midword by snarling, growling sounds.

"Get down," you whisper.

Lying on your stomach in the tall grass, you watch as two strange furry creatures holding clubs move toward you along the wall of the dam. They stop abruptly, turn, and walk away from you.

"Badders," whispers Sars. "I remember reading about them. They're mean cusses."

"What are they doing?" asks Chark.

"They seem to be guarding something," you say.

"They must be guarding the river wall," says Sars. "Look up the hill. They've built another wall forcing the river to make a loop."

"But why would they do that?" asks Chark.

"There must be something there they want to keep the river away from." You hesitate, then add, "Let's cross the stream and find out what it is."

Very quietly, so as not to attract the attention of the badder guards, you retrace your steps downstream until Chark finds a tree whose branches hang over the stream. Quickly he swings across. You and Sars hold on to low branches and make your way carefully over wet, slimy rocks in the streambed. Once on the opposite shore, you look up to see a large pond.

"Look!" you exclaim. "They've created a small lake. There's the old riverbed ahead of us."

"There's the reason they built the dam," says Sars.

"It's a whole village of badders!" you whisper. You drop to your stomach, thankful for the nasty-looking purple bushes that protect you.

You peer through the bushes and see a large group of domed huts. Small, furry badders scurry from hut to hut, frequently pausing beside a large fire.

"Looks like dinner time," sighs Chark, eyeing a badder as it walks away from the fire chomping on something.

"I'd like to get a closer look," you say.

"I can see just fine from here," says Chark. "Besides, what if we get caught?"

But you've already made up your mind. "We're going to crawl up to the next row of bushes. Stay low and keep quiet."

Without waiting for a response, you scramble forward to the next row of bushes and settle into the grass behind them. As you watch, you note that the sun has fallen farther behind the trees.

Now the badders seem to be preparing for the night. You can see large badders hurrying their little ones down ladders into the domes.

"Look there, off to the right," says Chark, pointing. "It looks like a cage."

"I can't see it," says Sars. "It's getting too dark."

"I can see it," you say. "Wait . . . they're pushing people into the cage!"

"By the way they're being pushed around, I don't think they're there by choice, either!" says Chark.

You continue to watch in silence. Several badders appear to be herding some human-oids into the cage. Suddenly one of the female prisoners stumbles. As she tries to regain her balance, a badder guard pushes her, sending her sprawling.

A tall, thin man nearby helps her to her feet, then whirls to shout at the badder.

"Can't you see that she can hardly walk?" he spits, towering over the badder. You see his face outlined in the light of the fire, his jaws clenched as he angrily brushes a lock of long red hair from his face.

"Isn't that—" you begin.

"It is! It's Jor!" Chark shouts.

"Shhh!" Sars hisses at him, but it's too late. The badder guard peers into the darkness toward you as you hold every muscle still. But the guard sees nothing and turns its attention back to the red-haired man.

With the back of one hand, the badder viciously strikes the man across the face. "That oughta teach you slaves who your mas-ters are," growls the badder.

Chin held high, the man continues to glare at the badder for a moment. Then he turns slowly and follows the woman into the cage.

The way the man moves rivets your attention. "It's Jor, all right. I'm sure of it," you say excitedly. "But he looks so thin and weak!"

1) If you think you should try to rescue your brother right away, in case the badders have nasty plans for him, turn to page 138.

2) If you think you should take more time to form a plan, turn to page 21.

"I can't bear to see my brother treated like an animal," you sputter. "Let's go!" You hold your spear at the ready and charge, not even sure if Chark and Sars are behind you. You dash blindly into the village, around the fire, and toward the cage.

Instantly, all activity stops. Hundreds of angry red eyes glare at you.

"Intruders!" voices cry, and dozens of the furry, growling creatures surround you and take away your spear.

Over the heads of the snarling badders, you see your brother pressing anxiously against the front of the cage.

"Ren!" he shouts. "Is it really you?"

"Jor!" you cry. "Are you all right?" You struggle uselessly against the arms that hold you.

"So you know each other, eh?" sneers the badder guard. It nods toward the two badders holding you. Grinning through pointy teeth, they shove you toward the fire.

"No! Not Ren!" you hear Jor scream.

Renewing your struggle, you twist one arm free of the badder claws. "Jor, we're here to—" Something heavy crashes down on your skull. Numb with pain, you struggle to keep from fainting.

Dimly you hear the slavemaster snarl, "Put him in the cage with the others!" and everything fades into blackness.

THE END

"We've got to fight or they'll get Chark for sure! Charge them!" you shout to Sars. You point your spear toward the attackers and dig your heels into your pineto's side. Sars moves in beside you.

As you charge down the hill on your galloping pineto, you see that Chark manages to snap to attention in time to pull his spear on the largest of the dog-men.

The mutant dogs don't know what to make of your spiny plant mounts. They hold their shields high and attack the tough plant steeds first, giving you a chance to use your spears. Wave after wave of the ferocious dog-men fall to your weapons, and for a while, you feel as if you may win.

But for every one you kill or drive off, two more of the barking dog-men appear in the sand. Soon your mounts are slain, and you are forced to stand and fight.

The blows of their clubs soon weaken you, and your spears are knocked out of your hands. All three of you are caught by the creatures. They put fur skins over your mouths and tie each of you to a long pole that they drag behind them as they march off into the hot desert.

THE END

"Maybe they can't see in the dark," you think. You and Chark grab Sars's arms and drag him into the tunnel. Walking with him in the middle, you slide your hand along the slimy, wet wall to guide you in your flight.

You hear a thump and a "Darn!" as Chark misses a turn and crashes into a wall.

"Use your hands to guide you," you say.

Sars tries to trust your guidance, but you sense him hesitating now and then. You push him on as quickly as you dare.

Suddenly, from ahead of you booms a loud, echoing voice that stops you in your tracks and sends you sprawling over Sars's foot to the cave floor.

"Who has come to disturb my rest? I see that you are not ants come to bother me again. Are you mutants?"

"What is it?" asks Chark.

"I don't know, but it sure doesn't sound like an ant," you say. You look over your shoulder and see no ants behind you—yet.

"It's waiting for a reply, Ren," Sars prompts.

You don't want this new unknown creature to become more upset, so you answer it.

"We didn't mean any harm . . . sir. We were just running from the ants and happened in here. We'd be happy to leave."

A beam of light blinds your eyes.

"You ARE human," the voice says with wonder. "Those ants attacked you? This cannot be! Please step aside, sir. I will deal with this and lead you and your pets to safety."

"Pets!" Sars exclaims angrily. "Does it mean us?"

"Shush!" Chark says. "The thing can call us bananas as long as it gets us out of here."

You all press close to the wall as you hear the sound of metal digging into earth and moving toward you.

A huge metal creature lights the tunnel ahead of you. As it nears, you see that it digs with a large scoop. It's definitely a machine of the Ancients.

As it turns into a side tunnel, it says, quite kindly, "I'm going to widen this tunnel so that we may all pass through it, sir. Please watch your step while walking behind me. I will light the way."

"It seems to like you because you're a pure strain human, Ren," Sars remarks. "I thought the Ancients weren't prejudiced."

"Don't look a gift pineto in the mouth," laughs Chark.

"Step lively now, sir," the machine says to you. "I can get you out of here, but you must stay by my diggers so these ants won't hurt you. Please keep your pets close by."

"Oh, he won't have any trouble with his pets, I can assure you," growls Chark as he pushes you and Sars closer to the machine.

Soon you again stand on the ledge above the crystal ant city. The whole place is alive with busy ants.

"The ledge surrounding the Crystal City is not wide enough for me," the machine says.

"Excuse me, sir, while I widen it." It begins to scoop at the wall.

Countless red warriors rush at you from the other side of the path. They try to bite the treads and shovel arms of the machine, but the machine just sweeps them aside and continues digging. The ants that aren't crushed are dashed to the roofs below.

"Look out!" Chark shouts. "There are more of them coming from the other way!"

Before you can even raise your weapons in defense, the machine's rear shovel arms sweep the huge ants off the ledge.

"I'm truly sorry if the warriors scared your pets, sir. Please do not worry. I will take care of everything."

You're not about to argue! You follow along, quite happy to let it lead.

Suddenly you see a horde of the red ants pour out of an opening on the far side. They start crawling up the sides of the cavern to reach you, plowing over anything that gets in their way — even other ants.

You're shocked. The sight of huge red warrior ants rampaging over each other and their beautiful city just to get at you fills you with disbelief. The ants seem like such a powerful force that you begin to wonder if this mighty machine of the Ancients can possibly push them all aside.

"Can't have this, can we, sir? I will take care of those troublemakers with a little hot asphalt."

A simply awful smell pours out of the machine. Then a stream of thick black liquid shoots out of several holes on the upper part of the machine. The black ooze covers the wall, the city, and the marching ants.

The determined ants keep trying to march, but the black stuff clutches at their feet until finally they can move only their frantically wiggling antennae.

"What IS that stuff?" you ask in awe.

"It is road tar, sir. I hope you don't object to using it in this critical situation. I know that it is a waste of public funds, but it seemed logical to use it. Please do not tell my supervisory unit. She is very cost conscious."

"We won't," you say, confused by the whole speech.

"Thank you, sir. We must hurry now," the machine says, and it resumes digging.

You follow it, and in a matter of moments you once again stand outside. There you see how large the machine really is. There isn't a house in your village half as big!

"Sir, I am concerned that the remaining ants will cause problems for other travelers. I must eliminate this potential problem. With your permission, I will return."

"Sure, go ahead. Have fun." You slap yourself on the forehead. What a dumb thing to say to a machine!

The machine disappears down the hole, pouring out some type of white liquid that begins to harden instantly, sealing the hole.

"You know, Ren, I never thought I would say this, but I almost feel sorry for all those big red ants," says Chark.

Sars flops in the shade of some rocks. "I'm exhausted. I can't walk another step." He punctuates his statement with a yawn.

"Maybe we should go farther away, just in case those ants get out," you say.

"I've seen those ants and I've seen your metal friend, Ren. I'm betting on the metal friend. Wake me when it's my turn to keep watch," Sars says, and promptly falls asleep.

"Go ahead and get some sleep, Ren," Chark offers kindly. "I'll keep watch."

You pat Chark gratefully on the shoulder, lie down, and drop into a dreamless sleep.

In the morning you discuss your choices.

"Although I found the red ant city fascinating, I think we should return to our original quest — finding the cause of the light on Quests Mountain," says Sars. "But my water's getting low. Let's stop at the oasis first."

"I think that we've gone too far not to find the airplane and explore it, if only to find out what one is," says Chark.

1) If you want to stop at the oasis, then head toward the mountaintop, turn to page 104.

2) If you decide to explore the airplane, turn to page 95.

You can't just serve poor Sars to this weird creature as if he were a lizard steak! He's your friend!

The orlen stands perfectly still, smiling at you as you whisper to Sars.

"Go right up to her, Sars. When you get near her, drop the cube. When she bends down to get it, use your spear. Chark and I will be right behind you."

"All right," Sars agrees hesitantly. "It was my cube that got us into this in the first place."

Sars's hand is still shaking as he walks slowly across the uneven cave floor toward the grinning creature. Three paces from the orlen, he pretends to stumble and drops the cube. It falls to the sandy floor of the cave with a dull plop.

"Ohhh," sighs the creature. Both its heads look down as the bottom set of arms reaches toward the cube.

You watch as Sars slowly reaches for his spear.

Suddenly the creature's left head snaps up and stares into Sars's frightened face. The top set of hands reaches for something on her right side.

"It can read my mind!" Sars shouts, panic in his voice. Staring straight into the eyes of the creature's left head, he starts to raise his spear. But out of nowhere, a huge four-handed sword flashes through the air and snaps the spear as if it were a toothpick.

Without thinking, you and Chark rush forward, your own spears pointed toward the two-headed figure. Twice more the huge sword flashes, and your spears fall to the cave floor, broken and useless.

"Run!" you shout, grabbing Chark's arm. Behind you, you hear Sars let out an earsplitting scream, and you hope he's following you through the tunnel.

You emerge into daylight and quickly turn to look back. There's no sign of Sars.

"Where's Sars?" you ask Chark frantically. "Where is he?"

Then you hear another piercing scream from the cave, followed by the creature's echoing laughter. Finally Sars stumbles headlong out the mouth of the cave, his glasses hanging loose off to one side.

"Didn't you hear me shout?" you demand, your concern making you angry. "Why didn't you run when we did?"

"I wanted to save the cube," he answers sheepishly.

"Never mind," you say, trying to calm your friend. You sit down on a rock to think. "We've got to figure things out. Our weapons are gone. We don't dare go back to the village without accomplishing something, especially after losing those spears." Your mind races as you grope for an answer.

Eventually the sounds of night creatures remind you that darkness is approaching fast. "Let's get away from this cave and find a

place to stay for the night." You yawn and stretch your tense limbs. Chark's mouth opens wide in a yawn of his own, and Sars tries hard not to do the same.

You've taken no more than two steps when you hear two frighteningly familiar voices, both speaking at once.

"The little boys are still here," says one. "Gooooood," says the other. You turn your head and see the weird shape of the orlen right behind you.

"Thank you for the pretty cube. Where did you get it?" the creature asks innocently, turning it round and round in her four hands.

With the memory of the creature's four-handed sword flashing through your mind, you waste no time answering. "My friend got it from his parents."

"We are not familiar with this place — this 'parents,'" one head says grimly. The smiles quickly fade from both heads.

"It's not a place. Parents are people," Sars says, then faintly mutters, "and I wish I were with them right now."

"So you will not tell us where to find the pretty cubes? We are not happy, are we?" one head asks the other. The second head shakes from side to side.

"We're telling you all we know!" you blurt. Suddenly you are seized with a great, unexplainable fear. Images of your family, the whole village, spin painfully through your mind and linger in a haze. You press your hands to your ears, trying to force the images to disappear. All of a sudden, you are aware of Chark's voice shattering your daymare.

"We have to go home! Something is terribly wrong!" His face is twisted in pain as his eyes plead for relief.

"The creature must be doing this!" sobs Sars, rocking back and forth in agony.

The images are so painful you can only stumble blindly into the forest, unaware of anything around you, with no thought except to escape from the pain. In your mindless flight, you dash through the unfamiliar forest as quickly as the darkness will allow.

Hampered by his night blindness, Sars stumbles and falls, then rises again, his step slowing to a limping walk.

The cries of pain of your two friends mingle with your own as you flee through the night.

The sun is rising as you emerge from the Green Lands a short distance from your village. As you break into a run, the images of pain become even more vivid. You must hurry! You must! You must!

You are met at the edge of New Hope by the outpost guards.

One grabs your arm. "Ren!" he cries.

You shake him off and rush through the gate toward your home. Your heart leaps when you spot your mother speaking with some village women in the square.

You rush up to her, dirty, bedraggled, and panting for breath.

"Ren! What on earth has happened?" This is not the heroic return that she expected.

Confused, you can only shake your head. You feel blessed relief as the images stop abruptly.

Your relief is short-lived as you hear a familiar voice behind you: "So this is parents. Gooood . . ."

Your knees buckle under you. The world around you grows dark, and you sink, exhausted, to the warm earth.

THE END

You look at both holes and say, "I'd rather take my chances with monsters that can fly to that top opening than ones that might have entered that lower opening. We'll go up," you say decisively.

Even using ropes from your packs, it's more of a struggle to climb up the airplane than you thought it would be.

"What could the Ancients have used this for?" you ask, gasping.

"I don't know," says Sars, "but one thing's sure—it's far too big to have been moved. It must have been built here."

The room you climb into is very small. Sunlight filters in through the hole, and you see dust clinging to every corner. There are three chairs with large mounds of white powder on them. The walls are covered with pieces of jagged see-through material much like that in Sars's glasses.

Looking through an open door, you see light streaming through many small windows above the walls of a very long room.

"This thing has been here a long time," Chark says, slightly worried.

"I wonder why it hasn't been disturbed before," you say. "Surely we aren't the first travelers to pass—"

CRASH! A door flings open at the far end of the long room, and three batlike monsters fly toward you!

You recognize these as obbs, creatures of the night that are well known in your village. You know that they swoop down out of the darkness and attack anything to satisfy their hunger. They eat only half of the victim's body and lay eggs in the rest of it. The eggs hatch in just three days, producing young that are ready immediately to attack and lay more eggs.

The ones coming toward you are young, moving slowly and rather clumsily, so maybe you stand a chance against them.

"The light bothers them," shouts Sars. "Get back by the hole where it's bright."

But there's no time! The obbs are on you!

Chark pulls his spear and stabs one, but another gashes Sars with its claws. You are able to kill it, but at the same time, the last of the three flies up to you, leaving you little room to maneuver. Chark jumps in front of you just in time to end the third obb's life with his spear.

You all breathe a sigh of relief and, encouraged by your success, decide to go on into the airplane.

You slowly stick your head through the door to the big room. It's even larger than you thought. Hundreds of chairs form long rows, and there's a small egg-shaped window next to every chair on the outside of the chamber.

"This must have been some type of meeting room," says Sars. "Maybe it was a school. But they must not have had much fun. Look at the straps in each seat."

"I hear something," says Chark. He stops

for a moment and shushes you both with a finger to his lips.

"There's a strange humming noise coming from the other side of that curtain down there," he whispers, pointing down a narrow path between two rows of seats.

"Let's not turn back now," you say more bravely than you feel. You walk forward with your spear held ready in front of you.

You reach the curtain and slowly slide the cloth to one side. You smell water.

You look down and find the source of the humming. One of the machines of the Ancients is still working.

Relieved, you take another step into the new chamber and promptly slip on the wet floor. Failing to catch yourself, you crash through an already broken structure and land in a pool of water!

Hearing a noise through your pain, you look up to see the body of a huge adult obb outlined in a bright white light.

You and Chark are frozen by the light, but Sars welcomes it. In one smooth motion he throws his spear into and through the body of the obb. The creature falls dead into the water, but still glows with light.

Finally, pain breaks through your fear. "Ow!" you shout. "Chark, Sars, help me. I think I broke my leg."

The other two drag you out of the water.

"Make sure that thing is dead," you tell Chark. "It shouldn't still be glowing."

"Ren," says Sars, "I've got to get you out of here. There might be more of those creatures."

Before you can object, he lifts you up in his strong arms, and the pain of your broken leg forces you into unconsciousness.

Hours later you wake up feverish. You're lying on a litter, being dragged out of the desert behind a pineto.

"Don't take these animals into our lands," you shout. "They'll die."

Your friends hurriedly dismount and try to quiet you.

"We've got to get you home," Sars says urgently. "Your leg is very bad. I did what I could, but it isn't enough."

"Nothing's more important than getting you back," agrees Chark.

The fever sends you into darkness again.

A long time later you wake up to find yourself a hero in your village! Your friends got you safely home and your leg is healing. Your father looks down at you, smiles with pride, and invites you to attend a meeting of the council of elders. When you get better, there will be plenty of time to solve the mystery of the light on Quests Mountain.

THE END

YOU LOVED THE BOOK.
YOU'LL BE DEVASTATED BY THE GAME!

Radioactive winds sweep across a devastated planet
Earth. Emerging from the charred debris is a monstrous
mutation bent on your destruction. What do you do?

Primitive and futuristic forces
collide in a battle for survival
in the science fantasy
GAMMA WORLD® game.

The GAMMA WORLD® game
includes a simplified rule-
book, campaign module and
a four-color two-sided map.
Get your GAMMA WORLD®
game today at toy, hobby
and gift stores everywhere!

™ TSR, Inc.
Products Of Your Imagination™

In the U.S.:	TSR, (UK) Ltd.
TSR, Inc.	The Mill, Rathmore Rd.
Box 756, C222EQB	Cambridge, ENGLAND
Lake Geneva, WI 53147	CB1 4AD

DUNGEONS & DRAGONS, GAMMA WORLD and PRODUCTS OF YOUR IMAGINA-
TION are trademarks owned by TSR, Inc. © 1983 TSR, Inc. All Rights Reserved.

ENDLESS QUEST™ Books

From the producers of the DUNGEONS & DRAGONS® Game

- **#1 DUNGEON OF DREAD**
- **#2 MOUNTAIN OF MIRRORS**
- **#3 PILLARS OF PENTEGARN**
- **#4 RETURN TO BROOKMERE**
- **#5 REVOLT OF THE DWARVES**
- **#6 REVENGE OF THE RAINBOW DRAGONS**
- **#7 HERO OF WASHINGTON SQUARE**
  based on the TOP SECRET® Game
- **#8 VILLAINS OF VOLTURNUS**
  based on the STAR FRONTIERS™ Game
- **#9 ROBBERS AND ROBOTS**
  based on the TOP SECRET® Game
- **#10 CIRCUS OF FEAR**
- **#11 SPELL OF THE WINTER WIZARD**
- **#12 LIGHT ON QUESTS MOUNTAIN**
  based on the GAMMA WORLD® Game

For a free catalog, write:
TSR Hobbies, Inc.
P.O. Box 756, Dept. EQB
Lake Geneva, WI 53147

TSR Hobbies, Inc.